Michaela Fink, Reimer Gronemeyer
Namibia's Children

Global Studies

Michaela Fink (Ph.D.), born in 1973, works as a research assistant at the Institute of Sociology at Justus-Liebig-University of Giessen; with experience in the field of African Studies since 2012 (focusing on Namibia, Malawi, Ethiopia). Since 2004, she has been a board member of the German NGO »Pallium – Research and Aid for Social Projects« that is supporting social projects in Namibia.

Reimer Gronemeyer, born in 1939, holds a Ph.D. in theology and in sociology. He is a Prof. em. at the Justus-Liebig-University of Giessen, honorary senator of the University of Giessen, and has conducted research in Zimbabwe, Sudan, Tansania, Namibia, Botswana, and Malawi. He is the chairperson of the German NGO »Pallium – Research and Aid for Social Projects«.

Michaela Fink, Reimer Gronemeyer

Namibia's Children

Living Conditions and Life Forces in a Society in Crisis

[transcript]

Bibliographic information published by the Deutsche Nationalbibliothek
The Deutsche Nationalbibliothek lists this publication in the Deutsche National-bibliografie; detailed bibliographic data are available in the Internet at http://dnb.d-nb.de

© 2021 transcript Verlag, Bielefeld

Cover layout: Maria Arndt, Bielefeld
Text layout: Wolfgang Polkowski
Cover illustration: Pietro Sutera, Children in the Havana soup kitchen, Namibia. www.pietro-sutera.de
Printed by Majuskel Medienproduktion GmbH, Wetzlar
Print-ISBN 978-3-8376-5667-1
PDF-ISBN 978-3-8394-5667-5
https://doi.org/10.14361/9783839456675

Contents

What is this about? An Overview

Many children in Namibia find themselves right in the centre of a social crisis. They have been abandoned, abused, are malnourished, homeless, or live in shacks that barely provide any protection. The surprising thing revealed in many talks with such children: Amidst these disastrous living conditions children develop remarkable survival skills, a strong will to live, and come up with equally clever and disillusioned analyses of their situation. It is mostly Namibian women who, in many different initiatives, build refuges for these children. These new environments are both saving and promising for the future in a society where traditional social cohesion (families, neighbourhoods, rural environments) are disintegrating.

For three years, the authors of this book conducted interviews in Namibia with women (and some men) who take care of vulnerable children. In interviews and essays these children were also able to voice their views.

The field work took place within the context of a three-year research project funded by the German Research Foundation (Deutsche Forschungsgemeinschaft). Throughout the interviews, from the first to the last of over one hundred, the confident vitality of the children was palpable. The women who have started soup kitchens, orphanages, kindergartens, and other initiatives, are people who, alongside the official national institutions, are creating a civic society, which acts locally, personally, unbureacratically, and with a lot of empathy.

The authors come from a brief analysis of the political and social situation in Namibia. The country which in 1990 (as the last country on the African continent) gained independence is full of contradictions. Rich in resources, peaceful despite its many ethnicities (and ethnic differences), with a free press, democratic elections, and a small basic state pension for old people, Namibia seems like an African model country. At the same time, Namibia is one of the countries where social inequality is most pronounced. Unemployment, alcoholism, and corruption characterise the daily life. The situation of children in particular has been deteriorating for years.[1]

This book is based on fieldwork from two Namibian hotspots:

On the one hand, in the smallholder agriculture region Oshana in the former Ovamboland. There, the characteristic local form of settlement, *egumbo*, is in crisis: Men have mostly abandoned the region to find work in the south. Traditional farming – not least because of climate change – is getting increasingly difficult.

On the other hand, in urban Katutura: the Black, in many cases informal settlement area of people who come from the rural areas to the urban region of Windhoek. Katutura, with its estimated several hundred thousand inhabitants, is already larger than the »old« »White« Windhoek.

The most important findings

In a 2011 report, UNICEF puts the *number of OVC* (orphans and vulnerable children) in Namibia at 250,000 (this equates to 26 per cent of all children and adolescents below the age of 18).[2] The 2011 population census states that a national average 13 per cent of all children and adolescents below the age of 18 were either half-orphans or full orphans (full orphans making up 2,7 per cent). The majority of orphans lost one or both of their parents as a result of the HIV/AIDS epidemic. Most orphans, in absolute numbers as well as in relative numbers to the high population density, lived in the rural regions in Namibia's North. In absolute numbers, out of 124,320 half-orphans and orphans 35,785

---

1   Cf. the Human Development Report 2013: 99; Melber 2015a.

2   UNIFEF 2011: 6.

lived in urban and 88,535 in rural regions.[3] Meanwhile, the findings of the interviews indicate that the situation is substantially more aggravated than what the official statistics show. For instance, a school principal in a village near Ondangwa reports that out of 365 pupils 120 are half-orphans or full orphans (roughly 33 per cent).[4] Not only the number of orphans but also the number of OVC in total is highest in the northern regions (Ohangwena 33 per cent, Caprivi 42 per cent, Omusati 34 per cent, Oshikoto 32 per cent, Kavango 31 per cent).[5]

Kinship care remains widespread in Namibia. That said, rapid modernisation processes alter this cultural practice. To many children, it appears utterly natural to live with relatives or other caretakers who are not their biological parents. The OVC crisis, which stems from the HIV/AIDS epidemic and the rapid dissolution of traditional family constellations, has on the one hand increased the necessity to take in non-biological children; at the same time, the willingness and material capability to take in children seems to decline.

The Namibian OVC expert and children's home director Rosa Namises believes that the African sense of community (*ubuntu*) is dying out. This would be evident in the constantly decreasing readiness of people to take in children and to take care of children in need.[6]

In the language of the Ovambo, the largest ethnic population group in Namibia, the cultural practice of giving away and taking in children is called *okutekulwa*. The Oshivambo word *okutekulwa* can be translated as *taming*. Children are given to grandmothers in particular.

Many orphans belong to the group of *vulnerable children* who need support and care. However, being an orphan does not necessarily equate to being undersupplied. Likewise, the group of vulnerable children also includes non-orphans whose parents are not able to take care

---

3   NPHC 2011: 55 et seq.

4   Interview with the principal, October 6, 2012, Ondangwa, Namibia.

5   MoHSS 2008: 258.

6   Namibian Sun 2019.

of their children – for example because they are alcoholics, sick, or live in extreme poverty.

Neglect and sexual abuse are fundamental experiences of many vulnerable children. Cultural traditions of politeness and obedience towards authorities make it difficult for boys and girls to resist harassment by authorities.

Although OVC are frequently taken in by relatives, compared to the biological children in the household they are often subject to *discriminatory treatment*, for example in terms of food or other forms of material support, in domestic work, or in school education. This discrimination also stems from the overload of families in difficult times. HIV-positive children or children who have lost a parent are often discriminated by their age peers and at times suffer from bullying at school.

Although the government gives out a small childcare allowance – the child welfare grant[7] – to children in difficult living conditions until the age of 18, many children never receive these monthly 250 Namibia Dollar. There are several reasons for this. Many children lack the necessary documents to apply for this grant (birth certificate, personal ID, or death certificate of their parent or parents). Sometimes families do not know of this national welfare programme. The registration is complex and protracted. Also, many people do not have the means to undertake the long journey to the proper ministry to go and register the child for the grant. Some also only speak their local language and not English, which is an additional obstacle. And it is not rare for legal guardians to embezzle the money which they receive from the state to cover expenses for the education of the child. Or it is difficult to get the money to the children: The grant is for example paid out to the father who works in the south while the child lives with an aunt in the north. In addition, the 250 Namibia dollar childcare allowance (approx. 16 USD) is far too

---

7   An overview of the child welfare grant in Namibia is available at: https://sister-namibiatest2014.files.wordpress.com/2016/11/child-welfare-grants-in-namibia-3_28.pdf.

little to support a child. Despite all these hurdles, the number of OVC who have registered for the grant has risen over the last years. While in 2016/17 285,431 OVC received it, in 2017/18 this number had already risen to 344,055.[8]

OVC struggle especially hard to graduate from *school*. Who pays for school uniforms and covers other school related expenses (like exam fees, hostel fees, transport expenses etc.)? School fees for visiting public schools were abolished in Namibia years ago (for primary levels in 2013, for secondary levels in 2016). However, against the background of the economic crisis many families fear that they might be reintroduced informally. OVC may officially be exempt from school fees, but in reality, they often struggle to prove their OVC status.

Corporeal punishment is widespread, it is regarded normal in many families and also common in school. In families – as our interviews and essays show – OVCs are punished more often than biological children.

Teenage pregnancies are frequent. Early sexual activities contribute to this, but it is also a result of rape, abuse, and prostitution. »Sugar daddies« seduce young girls with modern consumer goods. Girls from extremely poor families sometimes trade sex for money or food. In the Ohangwena region in the north of Namibia, where there is a lot of poverty, street construction workers, pastoralists, and border police officers are named among those who are involved in these consequential activities.

Baby dumping is often associated with teenage pregnancies, poverty, HIV/AIDS, alcoholism. There are places in Katutura, where social workers and police officers frequently looks for abandoned babies. Sometimes children whose mothers die in childbirth are also not picked up by their relatives, which can be regarded as a type of institutionally veiled baby dumping.

Many OVC suffer from *hunger or malnutrition*. The fact that food from traditional subsistence agriculture is being replaced by products

---

8   Namibian Sun 2019.

from supermarkets has a negative effect on the nutritional situation of these children since these wares have to be bought as well as because it leads to white flour and sugar replacing nutritious millet meals and vegetables. OVC for the most part neither possess sufficient nor balanced diets, proper clothing, to say nothing of their own money. 24 per cent of children below the age of 5 are stunted (low height-for-age), 6 per cent are wasted (low weight-for-height), and 13 per cent are underweight (low weight-for-age).[9]

Child headed households can be found in both urban and rural regions. Children in these circumstances often develop remarkable survival skills. They occasionally receive help from neighbours, friends, relatives, especially from older women. Still, their situation, particularly that of girls, remains difficult since they are unprotected in the face of male self-declared »guardians«.

Fathers – as well as men in general – do not play a big role in the education of children. It is rare for a child to be raised by their father. Men, in rural and urban areas, are mostly absent. They either work far away or live with another woman or are not interested in the child. This may at least partially be due to the fact that according to the Ovambo tradition children fall into their mothers' lineage.[10]

There is an unknown number of *street children*, who are not necessarily orphans. These children mostly come from extremely poor or destroyed families. There is a danger that they will become drug addicts or prostitutes. At times, street children form small groups who attempt to face the hardships of life on the streets together. These include children who may have a place to sleep somewhere with relatives, but who (have to) live on the streets during the day to earn a couple of dollar.

In both of the researched regions (in the Khomas and in the Oshana region) there are numerous *humanitarian activities*, who offer support for OVC. These initiatives are mostly led by women. Many of the ini-

---

9   The Namibian 2018a.

10   Cf. Brown 2007; 2011; 2013.

tiatives are called into existence by individuals, initially funded with their personal income, sometimes with a little support from the community or church. Only over time have some of these initiatives managed to find donors from within or without the country.

There are few *social workers* in Namibia. In the country with currently around 2,5 million people there were only approx. 500 qualified social workers were employed in 2015 country-wide.[11] Frequently, the social workers lack the necessary resources to work effectively.

The extended family is a central institution of Namibian society. As are the traditional authorities (headman, king, queen). With the emergence of the colonial, and since 1990 the postcolonial state, a new element has entered these ranks: the government. A new phenomenon in this regard are civil society initiatives, which emerge in social and societal gaps. It is debatable whether those initiatives, which target OVCs, could be counted as *civil society initiatives* (in the European sense of the term). If anything, their initiators (mostly women) likely view themselves more as people who are challenged by immediate destitution. They provide, one could argue, subsistent aid, which is initially removed from political and societal features – although the initiators heavily decry the failure of the state's aid programmes. These women do not regard their humanitarian initiatives as political actions. Barring a few exceptions, they do not view themselves as agents of societal change. They experience the state's actions as egotistic, bureaucratic, corrupt, and dominated by men. The mostly older women taken care of marginalised children, without initially intending for this to have political implications. Possibly, these initiatives functionally reproduce the old agrarian-familial environment as a refuge: The extended family, which lives together through conflict and harmony is the secret role model for these initiatives. This means that their primary inspiration is the traditional agrarian homestead *(egumbo)*, which makes a return in these initiatives. However, whenever international organisations or rather private humanitarian NGOs enter the picture, this changes

---

11   The Namibian 2015.

rapidly. The SOS Children's Villages are a prominent example of this process. Men take charge of things, »maternity« becomes organised. European or American standards for health, nutrition, and education dominate the situation. Initiatives turn into institutions. This has at least ambivalent consequences.

It is not entirely clear whether the women's initiatives are rooted primarily in traditional culture or if the women respond directly to the challenges of alarming life situations for children and to the effects of rapid modernisation. It is likely a mixture of both. What is a fact is that women, in many cases, guarantee social security, love, and warmth, whereas influential men in Namibian society tend to represent neoliberal, meritocratic standards.

The relation between government and civil society is difficult. The initiatives are mostly dependent on international donors who would like to exert control over how their money is used (often beyond the agreed upon regulations) and who sometimes try to assume management positions. This means that initiatives can fall into the hands of foreigners who then carry their own cultural norms into the initiative and, as experience has repeatedly shown, frequently care little about cultural perspectives and local circumstances.

At the same time, the national administration is trying to gain control over the initiatives and (via the setting of standards) to elevate them from the informal domain. Many initiatives, however, lack the resources to implement these standards. This is why some demand that the state should provide financial aid to help initiatives establish these standards.

While only officially registered OVC-institutions benefit from the meagre government funded child welfare grant (10 Namibia dollar per child and day in stationary institutions), the state is continuously expanding its control – and with it: bureaucracy – to all initiatives. The measures thus introduced often stem from ideas that were originally proposed by Euro-American experts only to then be adopted by the Namibian government and they frequently turn out to be difficult to implement for economic reasons. From the perspective of the state, the introduction of standards and control measures – against the background of the spreading of initiatives – serves as a necessary tool to exert control over the support of vulnerable children.[12]

Orphans and vulnerable children – who do we mean?

According to the official Namibian definition, children and adolescents below the age of 18 who have lost either both biological parents or one parent (or legal guardian) count as orphans. A vulnerable child is a child that is in need of special care and protection.[13]

Through the interviews it became very evident that in spite of the seemingly clear definitions the term »orphans« is problematic within the social and cultural context of Namibia. Put pointedly, one could say that the term is a construction of development and aid initiatives who work in Namibia and who have created the international definitions of OVC. Within the expansive scientific literature on the topic of »children and vulnerability in the context of HIV/AIDS« this Euro-American concept is discussed, presumed, or criticised. The term OVC has asserted itself in the contemporary global discourse of science and development cooperation and this has led to the creation of intervention measures, which respond to this concept. However, the number of authors who, in the context of the HIV/AIDS and orphan crisis, assume a critical position, which relativizes the vulnerability and trauma concepts, and who employ an anthropological perspective to shed light on the subjective experiences of OVC, remains low.[14] Again and again our interviewees emphasised that according to Namibian tradition there

12   For further information on the standards for RCCFs (residential child care facilities) see: MGWCW 2009a.

13   For a detailed elaboration see: MGECW 2007: 4.

14   Among others cf. Bray 2004; Cheney 2012; 2013; 2015; 2017; Crivello/Chuta 2013; Dahl 2009; Freidus 2011; Grothe 2015; Henderson 2006; 2012; Lancy 2008; Meintjes/Giese 2006.

are no »orphans« since all children are adopted by the extended family. Until today, the majority of OVC is taken in and cared for by the extended family. Indeed, one would have to say that the handling of children is more adequately described by the term »social parenthood«. Traditionally, the role of biological parents is peripheral. Among the Ovambo, aunts, grandmothers, namesakes *(mbushe)*, and older siblings[15] tend to be more prominent as care givers and the (time-limited or permanent) sending-away children to other locations and to other relatives was (and is) a cultural practice and normality. Newly wed couples, for example, were sometimes given a child »for starters«. Many children do not know and did not know in the beginning who their biological parents are because they consider, for example, their aunts as their biological mothers. In Oshiwambo, the term *okutekulwa* is used to describe this informal cultural practice of social parenthood. The term also refers to the »raising / growing up of children beyond their biological parents«. Important to this is and was the notion that it is better for children to be raised by people other than the biological parents.[16] Orphans within the cultural context of Namibia are therefore mostly regarded as a social phenomenon rather than a biological one.

The traditionally peripheral importance of biological parenthood can also be seen in the fact that until a few decades ago children used to exclusively address adults as *meme* and *tate* (mother and father). Only recently has a differentiation been observed where children also call adult relatives or non-relatives by the titles *aunty / uncle*, or *kuku / ouma* (aunt, uncle, grandma).

According to the population census of 2006/2007, only 25,8 per cent of all Namibian children below the age of 18 live with their bio-

---

15   Cf. Pauli 2015.

16   »Children could be sent out at very early age to homes where they are disciplined or where they learn a trade. Some parents are thought to spoil their children by not being firm on them, so sending them away is supposed to help them develop useful traits.« Isiugo-Abanihe 1984: 11. Most studies on child fostering focus on West Africa (like quoted here). However, there are many parallels to Southern African societies.

logical parents. 32,8 per cent live with their mothers, 5 per cent with their fathers, 36,4 per cent live neither with their biological father nor their biological mother.[17] (These numbers describe a tendency, however, with regards to the high household mobility they have to be considered a mere snapshot of affairs.) The migration of children between multiple caregivers, which our interviews as well as the pupil essays document, is only partially a result of the HIV/AIDS epidemic. The needs of children are considered in this circulation of children (children can demand to be returned if they do not feel well taken care of in their new household); however, the primary deciding factors of the sending-away of children in the tradition of *okutekulwa* (unlike in modern care and adoption regulations) are the necessities of the extended families and their households. This is the only way for households (especially in rural contexts) to persist. Sabine Klocke-Daffa examined the circulation of children as a form of informal social security using the example of the Nama people in Namibia.[18]

»Care« within the African context is not one-sided: Children are by no means mere passive receivers of care and support by adults. Children themselves take care of grandparents, sick people, younger siblings; they render domestic help, work in agriculture, and help in other forms of earning a living. Care circulates between generations.[19] Nevertheless, because of the AIDS epidemic responsibility is already weighing heavily on children. Eleven-year-old Anna from Katutura describes the situation that many children are confronted with: »There is no way that children just leave their parents lying around and say: ›Mom, dad, I am going to school now‹, while their parents are laying down and when they return from school they [the parents] are dead. The children have to take care of food, do washing. There are a lot of things to do to keep the household in order.«[20]

---

17   MoHSS 2008: 256.

18   Klocke-Daffa 2001.

19   Cf. Henderson 2012.

20   Interview with Anna E., 23.09.2013, Windhoek, Namibia.

The HIV/AIDS crisis has heavily contributed to a gradual change in the traditional caring practice because the increasing influx of orphaned children is overburdening the extended family. As a consequence, (AIDS-) orphans often receive worse treatment and care than biological children. Modernisation and migration processes are starting to erode the traditional extended family, individualisation processes begin to emerge (not just) among the elites. This has increased the importance of grandmothers even further – especially in rural areas. They are often responsible for a large number of children: Those are mostly grandchildren whose mothers and fathers have either died, work in the south (or are looking for work). Although it is part of the traditional role of grandmothers to take care of grandchildren, the sheer number of OVC is overburdening grandmothers. Their old-age pensions granted after the age of 60 (which currently lies at 1.300 Namibia dollar; approx. 87 USD) provide a small financial basis for survival. In rural areas, there is also the additional millet field. Many children – especially orphaned ones – are sent to the countryside, where life is more affordable than in the urban regions. According to UNICEF (2007), more than 60 per cent of all Namibian OVC are being raised by their grandmothers, especially in rural areas.[21] According to official guidelines, a child in the care of its grandmother lives in »alternative care« – in this case »kinship care«. From a local, cultural perspective, a child like this is not viewed as one that is growing up outside of its familial environment.

The pride that grandmothers take in having many grandchildren with them today is gradually giving way to the experience of being left alone with the childcare. »They dump their children with us.« This is a recurrent complaint by grandmothers, especially in the rural Namibia.

In the international development discourse there has been a terminological development with an opening of the term »AIDS-orphan« to the expanded term »OVC« (orphans and vulnerable children), or at times also »CABA« (children affected by AIDS), which can be regarded as a necessary response to the complexity of local realities. By now,

---

21   UNICEF 2007: 30.

the term »vulnerable children« has asserted itself as an umbrella term, which includes AIDS-orphans and CABA as one category of vulnerable children respectively. Within the research on AIDS-orphans there has also been an opening up towards other risk groups over the years.[22]

Vulnerable children, children in difficult living conditions, of which there are many in Namibia, are not necessarily orphans. Also, orphans are not necessarily AIDS-orphans. Many children are vulnerable children, because they are insufficiently cared for and protected, e.g. because their parents/guardians are sick, addicted to alcohol, homeless, and/or extremely poor; because the family is affected by crop failures or because children suffer from violence and abuse, or are victims of forced prostition or child trafficking, because they live on the streets etc.

In spite of this, many support measures in Namibia are aimed primarily at orphans which creates a complex situation in which various – governmental and non-governmental, national and international – actors are involved, all of whom presume a biological definition of the term »orphans« (instead of a social definition of orphans which would reflect the cultural notions and practices much better).

The mostly female initiators of OVC initiatives in Namibia take children from broken families: children of deceased or sick mothers, children of very young mothers, children from violent circumstances. These initiatives mostly persist on donations from foreign countries. There, the term orphans is differently connotated and understood, following the notion that children without biological parents are generally in need of help, which on the one hand helps raise the donation amount, but on the other hand also bestows a type of social reality upon the orphan status, which traditionally the term did not have. Orphans gain a special status, which did not use to exist in Namibia. Growing up with »social parents« was and is not viewed as an emergency solution, although »crisis fostering« (i.e. the taking in of children during crises) may always have existed.

---

22   Brizay 2011: 19–30.

Primarily though, the giving away of children was and is a cultural practice, which used to and continues to be widespread across many African countries.[23] In some African societies social parenthood was traditionally even the preferred form of parenthood, as the ethnologist Erdmute Alber was able to show using the example of West Africa (Benin). At the same time, this guardianship practice is subject to continuous change. As a consequence of modernisation and economisation processes biological parenthood has been gaining more importance.[24]

Within the matrilineal kinship system of the Ovambo (as well as among other ethnicities in Namibia) fathers only play a marginal role in the upbringing and support of children. In this sense, a child whose biological or social mother has died can basically be considered an orphan – though at the same time not, since the sisters of the mother are also *meme*, mother.

This being said, the burden imposed on families as a result of the HIV/AIDS pandemic has decreased the number of available foster mothers. Concerning the role of men, it is the brothers of the mother rather than the biological fathers who are considered responsible for the children. The migrant labour of men, which – as a consequence of colonial and post-colonial uneven development – has been affecting the social structure for generations and has fundamentally changed the relations between genders and generations, also contributes to the absence of many men.[25] In the rural and urban areas examined in our study many OVC are in the care of grandmothers and aunts. In the rural north as well as in urban Katutura men are rarely found alongside the women and children. Many of the women and mothers are single parents. In the north, in many of the cases where men have returned to the *egumbo*, the rural homestead, one can assume that they are so sick that they need help.

---

23   Cf. Gibbons 2013.

24   Cf. Alber 2013.

25   Cf. Schäfer 2004; Winterfeldt/Fox/Mufune 2000; Dilger 2005.

Aside from the »orphans label«, the »OVC label« is also ambivalent: On the one hand, it is appropriate to expand the term orphans and to include children from difficult life situations in the aid programmes. On the other hand, this also holds the danger that the term OVC may become »useful« inasmuch as it helps expand the clientele of charities: The number of the affected »grows« via the expansion of the target group, thus the government and non-government regulation tasks grow.

The necessity of such initiatives and national programmes is eye-catching but the existence of rescue options also fuels an increasing »demand«. Nevertheless, pregnancies among pupils, prostitution, alcohol, and HIV-infections drive more and more (single) women to situations in which they are not able to look after their children. In a process consisting of the erosion of traditional family structures, individualising modernisation, and increasing weakness of agrarian subsistence, the phenomenon of orphans is, in a sense, created, while initiatives take both a helping and a reinforcing role.[26] Finally, it becomes difficult to tell apart cause and effect in terms of the social phenomenon »orphans«. What does however become evident is an increasing normative disruption of the Namibian society, of which the children of the poor in rural and the urban areas in particular are victims.

In many households, there is not enough money (nor enough harvest) to get food to satisfy everyone. Extremely long ways to school are normal in the north, which considering that many children eat one meal of *oshifima* (traditional millet porridge) per day, leads to exhausted pupils who frequently fall asleep during school. Helping out in the household or in the agriculture is considered natural by many children.

The nutritional situation of OVC is apparently worsening. The traditional subsistence nutrition on the countryside, which used to be characterised by millet porridge as a basis along with different types of vegetables, fruits, and chicken, is thinned out, also because fewer men (due to their absence) and children (due to them being in school and often living in hostels) are available for tending to the fields and

---

26   Cf. Cheney 2013: 155.

cattle. Additionally, fast food and soft drinks exert a certain fascina-
tion on the local populace. This is not without consequence on the nutritional status. Official data puts the number of Namibian children
who die due to under- and malnourishment at 6,000 per annum.[27] The
nutritional situation of the countryside is continually worsening. Lack
of money makes it impossible to buy enough food.

The interviews with pupils as well as the pupil essays reveal that
(AIDS-)orphans still frequently experience discrimination. It is often
reported that orphans are put under suspicions of being infected with
AIDS themselves, which leads to them being humiliated within their
families and at school. OVC suffer more frequently than other children from corporeal punishment. Corporeal punishment of children
is widely regarded as normal.

The extent of child abuse, especially rape through male relatives,
is alarming although the dark figure in this regard prevents any exact
estimates.[28] The national average for teenage pregnancies lies at 15,4
percent – in the northern region of Caprivi even at 34 per cent.[29] The
principal of a bush school in the northern Ohangwena region reports
that the number rises whenever street workers who flatten the sand
roads were in the vicinity. Only rarely are the child fathers school-
mates, or other same-age people. Usually it is older men with monetary incomes[30], which suggests economic motives on the side of the
girls. Often it is sheer plight that forces girls to sell their body. The men
pay schoolgirls a few Namibia dollar. There are also frequent reports
of sexual relationships between female students and teachers. Sometimes parents welcome relationships like this, says the principal, if the

---

27   Cf. NAFIN 2010: 5.

28   According to the Legal Assistance Center (LAC), there are 45 reported cases of
      rape per 100.000 adolescents annually. Compared to other so-called developing
      countries, this Namibian figure is above average. See: Legal Assistance Center
      (2006): 3–4.

29   NAFIN: 29.

30   The Namibian 2014.

teacher supports the family of the girl. OVC are also affected the strongest by commercial child trafficking, as the »Trafficking in Persons Report 2010« states: »Namibian women and children, including orphans, from rural areas are the most vulnerable to trafficking.«[31]

Gender-based violence (GBV), a topic that has been making headlines in Namibia for several years, is also primarily directed against women and children. In this case as well, OVC are particularly threatened. The violence is usually domestic and with increasing frequency leads to so-called »love killings / passion killings«: »Namibia is battling a scourge of passion killings and brutal rapes, including those of the minors,«[32] writes the newspaper »Namibian Sun«. On March 6, 2014, former president Sam Nujoma declared a National Day of Prayer against GBV. Our interviewees mostly described GBV as a modern phenomenon that is connected with the increasing monetisation of relationships as well as with uneven power relations between men and women. Greed, jealousy, alcohol, and drug abuse are named as concrete causes – along with the loss of traditional male role models: Men nowadays are often incapable of economically providing for their family. This can cause feelings of inferiority and create fragile self-consciousness, which, especially under the influence of alcohol and drugs, can turn to violence. According to official crime statistics, between 2009-2013 an annual average of 48 women (and 204 men) were murdered. The offenders are mostly young men in their twenties.[33]

---

31   Trafficking in Persons Report 2010: 244.

32   Namibian Sun 2014.

33   The Economist 2014; also see: Namibian Sun 2016.

I. Children of the Crisis –
Living Conditions in Namibia

A simple life

Huge dark eyes, flies settling down on their crusted edges, children with hunger edema on cracked, dried up land, White doctors and nurses, who lean above sick or malnourished babies: icons of the press reportage on children in Africa. Clichés, however, such photos and reports are not conjured from thin air, but time and again describe the reality at the focal points of flight, famine, war, and natural catastrophes on the African continent. They indicate the number of children that starve, suffer from malnutrition, and who remain physically or mentally underdeveloped as a consequence of food shortages.

The pertinent studies and reports offer numbers and data, behind which hides a bitter reality, a daily suffering. This squalor, growing in some places, already habitual in others, is also evidenced by the number of babies abandoned by their desperate, sick or alcohol-addicted mothers. Children who work in the cobalt mines; children who have been turned into soldiers: children in crisis. This book deals with the everyday misery of children in Namibia. It is about hunger, violence, abuse, neglect, homelessness, powerlessness, and the experience of unkindness. We will describe the devastation of social coherences, during which children are growing up these days, shed light on the social wreckages over which these children stumble and on which they try to survive. But this is only one facet of reality, the dark side. We also want to draw attention to an entirely different phenomenon: to the remarkable strength and vitality of African children which shines through, despite and because of situations of daily poverty, widespread malnutrition, and destroyed living conditions.

The life of these children is a simple one: it is about the bowl of millet porridge, which they hope to get; it is about water that has to be fetched; it is about the contribution that children are expected to render on the millet field, with tending to the goats, or with cooking the porridge; it is about the grandmother who cares; it is perhaps about the father who is a drunkard or the mother who works hundreds of kilometres away; it is about the difficulty of graduating from school. Simple, mundane questions of survival. Questions to which, for the most part, European children are strangers. Italian novelist Pier Paolo Pasolini spoke of the »Age of Bread« with regards to old rural Italy: Not a golden age but an epoch during which people led modest, mostly reliable self-sufficient lives.[34] This description still holds true for the life situations of many people, especially children, in Namibia. That being said, the old, subsistent, agrarian environment has been corroded and damaged. The modest agrarian life has become a fragile setting from which former rural dependabilities have vanished.

Usually, shifting the perspective towards the agrarian living conditions immediately prompts suspicions of romanticising. »Retrogression, cultural pessimism«, exclaim those who are enslaved by a monoculture of thinking which can only ever look forward; which severs ties to all heritage, all memory; which is trapped in total contemporaneity and has carried out a complete break with the past, which is deemed irrelevant.

The popular accusation of »social romanticism«: Does it not ultimately reveal a feeling of superiority by contemporary culture towards all of the past? Does it not bespeak a contempt for everything, which does not submit to the logic of growth, of economic efficiency and utility? Let us be frank: It is difficult to withstand this logic. We may be ever so interested in traditional societies. Deep down, however, we do not believe that they have anything essential to contribute to the

---

34   Pasolini 1989: 55 (Pasolini refers to an expression by Chilanti).

modern world.[35] Still, we should be careful not to dismiss the agrarian, subsistence-focused worldview as primitive. After all, the agrarian treatment of the world has done less harm to the planet than what the modern human does with their infinitely grown possibilities.

Many Namibian children, no matter if they live in rural or urban environments, find themselves in precarious conditions. The children of the elites and small middle class, on the other hand, are already part of a modern consumerist living environment, which mainly emerges in the capital Windhoek. As a consequence of modernisation, migration, war, and diseases (particularly the HIV/AIDS epidemic), traditional living conditions which on the countryside used to provide food, shelter, and extended familial protection have been severely damaged, in some places even utterly dissolved. Additionally, the obvious effects of climate change are especially palpable in Namibia – they are evident in both droughts and floods. Following a severe drought, in 2020 Namibia is suddenly beset by floods. For Southern Africa, experts prognosticate an increase in temperature of five degrees Celsius or more.[36] According to data by the World Food Programme, 25 to 34,9 per cent of Namibia's population suffered from malnutrition in the years between 2016 and 2018.[37] For 2019, this number is likely to be even higher.

Many international donor organisations have withdrawn from Namibia since 2009 when the World Bank declared Namibia a middle-income country, and thus catapulted them out of the ranks of countries in need.[38] While indeed, the average incomes have increased, it is also true that the situation for poorer parts of the population have worsened both in relative and absolute terms. This is mainly connected to increased living expenses, critical developments in families, and to the social impact of the HIV and AIDS epidemic. State-funded social

---

35   Cf. Fink 2019: 138.

36   BBC News 2019.

37   WFP 2019.

38   Cf. Melber 2018: 6; for information of the sociopolitical history of Namibia after the independence see Melber 2015b.

benefits (child welfare grant, disability grant, and old age pension) are institutionalised (albeit connected with major bureaucratic hurdles); however these benefits are insufficient due to the massively dwindling purchasing power. Additionally, the income distribution is extremely uneven.[39]

The situation of many children in Namibia is dramatic. In rural areas, the smallfarm-based food supply is crumbling away (climate change, rural exodus, labour migration). In urban areas, poor shack households, in which women with their children mostly try keep house themselves, are predominant. People in such situations are often precariously close to being malnourished, they dwell beneath haphazardly mended roofs, they sleep on shabby mattresses. One bed for the entire family is not uncommon. If many children live in a household, some have to sleep on the floor.

And in spite of all this, there is this power and intensity which almost constantly emanates from the children. Although they live in what appears to us as fragile family relations, although the walk barefoot, although they hardly have any toys, although many are beaten, or (by our standards) neglected. Perhaps – and this is what shall be examined in the following – the secret of their overflowing vitality actually lies in the very conditions which to our views appear fragile. One has to be wide awake to persist under these circumstances.

Traditionally, children in Southern Africa do not grow up in small families (that trend is only now beginning to become a reality for the urban elites). The sisters of the mother are regarded as mothers. The relation between the biological mother and the child is – traditionally – not exclusive. The role of father in traditional settings used to be a rather distant one. Today, fathers are often absent. Many have disappeared entirely (»they don't support«) or they are absent due to labour migration. Namibian children in rural and urban area are in an unenviable position: And yet they move like fish in the waters of a highly

---

39   See the country overview on Namibia on the website of the World Bank: https://www.worldbank.org/en/country/namibia/overview.

In spite of modest and often difficult living conditions, many children exude remarkable vigour and zest for life.

flexibilised living environment where secure family circumstances are just as rare as reliable nutrition or solid shelter.

Our assumption is that this flexibility with which Namibian children live, along with the plethora of daily challenges they must face, evokes a powerful wakefulness in them. They are also largely outside of any consumer culture whose paralysing and numbing effects can be observed in children from Western civilisations. Once again, to reemphasise: This is not meant to whitewash the misery and plight of these children. It is, however, becoming evident that the mixture of remnants of African traditions, of the daily challenge of dealing with paucity, of the necessity to be flexible and to improvise, that all of these together do something special to the children. The concentrated simplicity of living conditions brings with it an unusual vitality and zest for life. These children are not as intimidated, apathetic, not as unimaginative, nor as afraid of life as our prejudices would have us believe.

A good example is Selma. She has been walking for one hour on foot when she arrives at her school deep within the bush of northern Namibia. Prior to leaving for school she already walked a path while balancing a plastic bucket full of water on her head: She left her hut to fetch the water needed for cooking, drinking, and washing from the well. Now she is sitting in the classroom and pulls up her booklet and book. When school finishes in the afternoon, she and the other children receive a bowl of maize porridge, which has been prepared by voluntary helpers from the village in huge kettles. This is the first time she eats on this day. It is a modest meal, but for many it is the only reliable meal per day. The children sit by themselves or in groups on the floor and with nimble hands scoop up the porridge from the bowl. Hardly anyone speaks during the meal: This occasion is too important and anticipated. After school, she will walk back to the hut of her family. There she will lend her grandmother a hand and do her homework.

It is – as mentioned before – a simple life with great daily challenges, and in which the basics of life matter. Still: No matter who we talk to – these children exude energy and vitality. Although – compared to our European conditions – they should have reason for lament.

What we present here are the results of years of fieldwork in Namibia, which – funded by the German Research Foundation – mainly took place between 2012 and 2015. The results of this this were complemented with further research stays in this country which still continue to this day, and which yielded additional interviews and insights. This includes the practical cooperation with Namibian children's aid projects that emerged from the field research.[40]

---

40   Between 2000 to 2004, Reimer Gronemeyer (together with Georgia A. Rakelmann, Matthias Rompel, and Marco Schäfer) conducted a DFG project on the »social impact of HIV/AIDS in Botswana and Namibia«. A project funded by the Fritz Thyssen Foundation (Reimer Gronemeyer together with Daniela Dohr, Philipp Kumria, and Jonas Metzger) on the topic »Seed systems and social structures. Food security in rural development areas in the Oshana Region/Namibia and the Ruvuma Region/Tanzania« was conducted between 2011 and 2013. From 2012 until 2015, Reimer Gronemeyer and Michaela Fink researched the ways in which Namibia deals with orphans and vulnerable children within the context of the DFG project that forms the basis of this book.

But before we begin to describe the situation of children in rural areas on the one hand and in urban areas on the other hand, some preliminary considerations deserve elaboration. The question that needs to be asked is: How is possible to write about African living conditions from Europe without getting entangled in a mess of misunderstandings? Is this yet another reiteration of White dominance, which once again presumes to explain to Africans who they are, what they do wrong, and what they should be doing?

Writing about Africa? Postcolonial hesitancy

Those who dare to write about Africa will find a field where every single word has become problematic. Is not the term »Africa« already a generalisation, the likes of which are only possible from a European perspective? Does using it not bear the resonance of colonial perspectives, from which the continental bustle of states and ethnicities was simply lumped together under one term? After all: What do Algerian Berbers have to do with Namibian Herero? Or Nigerian Yoruba with Ethiopian Oromo? »Africa« – that is a word, a term, which in Europe is mainly good for evoking clichés. The starving child with the thin legs; the lion that kills the zebra; the sunset in the bush; the child labour in cobalt mines.

Kenyan novelist Binyavanga Wainaina gave ironic tips, on how to write about Africa from a European perspective:

These projects were conducted at the Institute of Sociology at Justus-Liebig-University Giessen and each contained multiple months-long fieldwork stays. Additional sources for the present book were connected to the work by authors Reimer Gronemeyer and Michaela Fink in the charitable organisation »Pallium – Research and Aid for social Projects«, which supports aid projects (especially ones for orphans and vulnerable children) in Namibia. From these research projects, the following publications emerged (among others): Gronemeyer 2005; 2007; Fink/Gronemeyer 2015; Dohr/Kumria/Metzger 2015.

»Among your characters you must always include The Starving African, who wanders the refugee camp nearly naked, and waits for the benevolence of the West. Her children have flies on their eyelids and pot bellies, and her breasts are flat and empty. She must look utterly helpless. She can have no past, no history; such diversions ruin the dramatic moment. [...] And end your book always with Nelson Mandela saying something about rainbows or renaissances.«[41]

The thoughtless cliché and the brutal reality often come frighteningly close to each other. In that sense, it is a difficult, delicate task to write about African conditions. Colonial arrogance lurks beneath each word.

»Whiteness is more than a skin colour, it is a social position, a stance, and an interpretive pattern. White dominance is evident in the consumption of resources, in economic power and money flows, in the interpretation of conflicts, in the writing of history. In these fields we are witnessing the dawn of a new age. The West no longer determines the order of the world and we can no longer force our definitions of progress, development, or feminism onto others.«[42]

In this vein, Charlotte Wiedemann writes in her book of the »parting from white dominance«. This is correct, but upon closer inspection, several questions emerge. Does this also mean that Europeans have to keep silent when it comes to the widespread practice of female genital mutilation? Do we have to remain silent on the fact that in 78 countries, roughly half of them in Africa, prosecute homosexuality as a criminal offense and that in Sudan it is even punishable by death?[43] In November 2019, the Namibian ministers of justice and fishing stepped down because, according to a whistleblower, they had allegedly taken bribes from the Icelandic fishing company Samherji. Now, of course,

41   Wainaina (2005).

42   Wiedemann 2019: 10 (own translation of the quote).

43   Die Presse 2014.

the Iceland-case also reveals that White dominance in many cases is what paves the way for corruption in the first place. Then again, Frantz Fanon, pioneer of the anticolonial resistance, already bitterly bemoaned the devastating corruption in 1961:

> »It is an irony of history that our limitless solidarity not only blinded us to the crimes committed in the name of the fight for freedom but also to the return of colonial power structures. After the independence, the black masters leapt into the silken beds and swimming pools of the white masters and exploited their peoples just like them.«[44]

Colonialism, one could argue, has a certain infectiousness.

Against which standard do we measure? And who does the measuring? The respect for African culture also has to be maintained in areas where African ways of life do not agree with our European ones. But are there limits to this? Does the European Convention on Human Rights also apply to a village in Uganda? Is the »Universal Declaration of Human Rights«, adopted by the UN General Assembly in 1948, an instrument of White dominance? Have White people – after the trail of blood left by the slave trade and colonialism – lost their right to criticism? Should they not rather mind their own business? Especially considering the impending postcolonial catastrophe that is climate change, which is chiefly caused by the global North while its consequences so far mainly have to be borne by the global South, particularly Sub-Saharan Africa? Will the climate catastrophe outdo even the slave trade and colonialism in terms of harm inflicted upon Africans? Who then has morality on their side? And why should Europeans retain the right to point fingers at Africans and hold them accountable?[45]

The Afro-American novelist and laureate of the Nobel Prize in Literature Toni Morrison challenged people to reverse the perspective and look at the people who create racist hierarchies or marginalise oth-

---

44 Quoted in Grill 2019: 11 et seq (own translation of the quote).
45 Cf. Menke/Pollmann 2007.

ers.[46] Peggy McIntosh, an Afro-American educational scientist, spoke of the, »invisible backpack which white people carry with them,« and she sarcastically described this backpack, for example, with a sentence only White people could say: »I can be late to a meeting without having the lateness reflect on my race.«[47]

When writing about Africa from our part of the world we must not abstract colonial history. We must refrain from any know-it-all attitudes.[48] But we can attempt to empathically and humbly write about that which is observable in »Africa«: Touched by their pain, we can report about vulnerable children. And, at the same time, we can be awed by these children who, from rickety shacks, in front of empty cooking pots, on endlessly long ways to school, and in destroyed families, begin to comprehend their lives with an incredible power, clarity – and yes, even merriment.

In this book, we attempt to trace this ambivalent picture: How do these »children of the crisis« live and survive? And we try to retell how women in Namibia (which is where we conducted our fieldwork) with determination and bravery, without monetary cushions, and without outside support, pick themselves up and create refuges for these vulnerable children. We try shed White domination patterns in this book and we do this by first and foremost listening to the voices of Black children, while also listening to women, who are their »caretakers«, and thus have daily first-hand experiences with how bad the children's living conditions are. Women who are outraged by the lethargy of the population, by the apathy of the authorities – and by the violence, which men in the country especially bring to bear against them.

---

46   Garschagen 2015.

47   McIntosh 1988: 4. The author compiles »daily effects of white privilege«; see https://projecthumanities.asu.edu/content/white-privilege-checklist.

48   Jamaican philosopher Silvia Wynter posits that the category of the human(e) is a narrative which was fabricated by European men for European men. In opposition to this, Wynter develops a theory of »counterhumanism«, quoted in: Avanessian/Moalemi 2018: 84.

In the newspapers reports of rape and the abuse of children pile up: Is Namibia a society whose ethical foundation is in a process of dissolution? Rosa Namises, former member of parliament, Chief of the/ Khomanin people, director of »Woman Solidarity Namibia« – called the »Rosa Luxemburg of Namibia« – manages the Dolam Children's Home, where vulnerable children live. Faced with the reports about an abused and murdered girl and about the rise of abuse and violence against children in Namibia, she expresses her outrage:

> »As I said all the time, and I'm still going to say it: Men have declared war against women. Not only against women – we need to say it very specifically: against little girls, against elderly, against little boys. And that is a very horrific and scary action. I think, we would want to say ›the way they are raised... maybe there was no family frame work, in which we have to sit down and raise our boys‹. I could have said that, but the men, who are committing that crime are men that was supposed to be raised already in the 70s and in the 60s, because their age is quiet high. A 50 year old man, a 70 year old man, those men are supposed to be growing up in a time where we don't need to blame independence. And therefore, the moral decay of our society speaks a lot at the moment. [...] I am also saying to myself in my little corner: What will I ever do, if I find the culprit right on the scene? It's only my adrenaline that can talk about it. But for me, the actions that we need to take is to start standing up together. [...] who are the majority voters in this land? To make them safe is important. Let there be a call to declare this violence as an emergency in this land of ours. Or even, just the ministry of that matter to just declare that we have an emergency situation. I'm calling also on the men, who are peaceful, who have that little respect left for us, to stand up as one voice! I see them there, when we act. Like I saw them in the community. So I know that there are men out there, who

really want this not to happen. And I'm asking them to start to move on, to come on board, so that we can fight this together.«[49]

Does Rosa Namises exaggerate? Is the situation of children and women in Namibia really this dramatic? In March 2016, the UNO presented the results of an investigation into the human rights situation in Namibia and came to the conclusion that discrimination and abuse of women and children are everyday occurrences.[50] There are of course countries where the situation is worse than in Namibia. But for a country with functional democratic institutions; a country with many legal rights meant to protect children and women; a country which in 1990 began its independence with a number of passionate programmes for a new social justice – the results are sobering. An investigation in the Hadap region in 2015 found that 80 per cent of 100 interviewed girls between the ages 15 to 19 had had either direct or indirect experiences with physical violence. Likely connected to this is another frightening number: Out of 5,400 interviewed children, 26,6 per cent had attempted suicide in the past six months.[51] Though this is a regional snapshot, it still gives an idea as to the sometimes desperate situation of young people in Namibia.

Figures, figures, figures: While they inform readers, they also risk leaving readers emotionally unaffected. This is why we choose to begin with the voice of a woman from urban Namibia, who illustrates the environment in which many children in Namibia grow up today and who emphasises the frequently catastrophical situation of children.

---

49   »It's a wrap: child rape reports in the rise.« Interview with Rosa Namises in »One
      Africa«, 13.09.2019. https://www.youtube.com/watch?v=4YX0BU_9QqU.
      On the phenomenon of Gender-Based-Violence in post conflict societies see e.g.
      Manjoo/McRaith 2011 and Edwards-Jauch 2016.

50   The UN report is quoted by Hofmann 2016.

51   Ibid.; cf. also Mel 2015.

Hileni: a voice from Katutura [52]

»Those who feel as human will be unhappy about many humane things, but be in harmony with themselves. This, I believe, is how happiness and commitment belong together.«
(Eugen Drewermann, German theologican, in a speech upon receiving the Erich Fromm Award in 2007)

Hileni knows the fringes of Namibian society well. She takes care of children who live in a particularly poor urban shack settlement. Shanties constructed from sheet of metal, naked earth, a bed, a pot on an open fireplace, no electricity, no water – a common picture that is predominant across the informal settlements of this world. This goes without saying: no toilet, sometimes a plastic sheet behind which one can pour a bucket of water over their head. Women with children, women without work. Men who are huddled together in front of huts and drink *tombo*, the homebrewed beer. Hileni estimates the number of people in the shantytown who pursue a formal job to be around 10 per cent. Ten per cent who work e.g. as security guards, gardeners, employees in hotels, restaurants, or supermarkets, as newspaper vendors, or cab drivers in the city centre of Windhoek. Many people attempt to make a living through informal work within the township: Women sell self-baked bread, fatcakes, grilled meat (kapana), fruits, and vegetables at small stalls. Or they work as laundresses for neighbours, take care of children for a small fee. Some women view prostitution as the only chance to survive. Day labouring is mostly done by men.

Hileni paints a bleak picture: She speaks of daily conditions that are getting worse from her perspective. Thanks to Hileni, more than 40 vulnerable children in pre-school ages receive 2 meals per day – breakfast and lunch. Additionally, Hileni manages a programme which sup-

---

52   The telephone interview was conducted by Michaela Fink in November of 2019. The name has been changed per the interviewee's request. The interview was anonymised completely for publication.

plies some of the poorest household in a shack settlement with food and other everyday necessities. Elderly people and sick ones in particular receive food, milk powder for their babies, blankets, winter clothing, plastic sheets to cover their leaky huts, as well as medical services and help with paying for funerals etc.

Hileni's small initiative is situated in one of the poorest parts of Katutura. Katutura is a district of Windhoek, Namibia's capital. No, actually it is not a district of Windhoek. Katutura was founded in 1950 as a suburb of Windhoek. This means that Katutura was created in times of Apartheid, when Black people were needed as a labour force but not supposed to live in White Windhoek and therefore outsourced to Katutura. In times of rural exodus Katutura is growing. In 2019 the number of inhabitants is estimates to be in the hundreds of thousands. The suburb for labourers has become an uncontrollably growing colossus, which by now towers over old Windhoek. Vibrant, diverse, creative, is what Katutura is like, but at the same time also characterised in vast parts by poverty and unemployment. Corrugated-iron shacks characterise the townscape (which is why the townsfolk have taken to calling it »silvertown«). The administration in Windhoek cannot keep up with the wild growth, and again and again has to reluctantly acknowledge the status of squatter settlements. The transition from informal to formal settlements brings with it building regulations as well as resettlements. But it also slowly drives forward the connection to the electricity networks, water supply, and sewers.

People come to us with tears in their eyes...

Hileni says: »Here in Namibia, we are in a dramatical economic crisis. The economy is in bad shape. People, even here in the city, are suffering from the drought [this was in 2019] because the supply chain from the countryside has been cut off. Many people who come to me get to the most important question straight away: They have already contacted the authorities but those had no solutions to offer for their problems, they say. This is why they come to me. And they come with all kinds of problems, hoping that I can help them.

People of all ages come to me: young women with children tied to their backs, elderly women and men. They come with tears in their eyes. I have to be very strong. And some of them come with terrifying stories. Why do these people come? The number one reason is ›poverty‹, number two is ›hopeless poverty‹. Many of the people who seek out my initiative want me to take a look at their hut so that I can get a clear picture of their difficult living situation. They suffer a lot from stress. They say: ›You can even ask my neighbours how I live. I have children and I am hungry.‹ Some of them say: ›Touch my belly and you will see that I have not had a thing to eat for one and a half days. I went to the government offices and did not receive any Harambee.‹ [*Harambee* is something similar to a food bank where the poorest people sometimes receive food from the state.][53] What the people do, however, tell me is that the government officials take what they get for distribution and give it to their own families.

The people who come to me say: ›Look, Hileni, it is better to die. It is better to commit suicide.‹ And I respond: ›No, that is not a solution!‹ They say: ›What do I have to live for? Come and take a look at my hut and my situation.‹ Sometimes people tell me things in confidence: Things that I do not even want to talk about anonymously because they are that terrible. But one example that I can talk about: The people in our shanty town do not have toilets. There are only very few public toilets here and the area is huge. And, you know, if you live in the middle of the settlement and have to go to the toilet, where do you go? What people do is they use a plastic bag. They take their plastic bag, shopping bag, whatever. And that's where they put everything. [...] The situation of many people is so bad that they think dying is the only solution. In this part of Katutura the suicide rate is very high.

---

53   The Harambee Prosperity Plan was declared on April 5, 2016, by Namibian president Hage Geingob.

I have brought this up with the police. They are not on good terms with us, with the poor people. Recently, we had a small accident in our settlement. I went to the police. And while I was at the station, a woman with a very small baby came in. I think the baby must have been about two months old. She came in and she was bleeding. She told them that there had been an altercation with her boyfriend and that he had hit her. She said that he had even thrown the baby onto the floor and that she didn't know what the condition of the baby was now. And then, in front of my eyes, the police asked the woman: ›So, what do you suppose we should do about that? Do you have 800 [Namibia] dollar for an ambulance? If you don't, we can't help you.‹ I couldn't really interfere with the conversation because I was there on different business. I was baffled. But after I left the police station tears came to my eyes. I couldn't control myself anymore. To see this small baby in the arms of her bleeding mother – and the police tell her that she needs to have 800 dollar. This woman – and you could see that – was the kind of person who didn't even have 10 dollar to buy a fatcake. This really outraged me. I was so confused that I nearly ran into a car that passed me by. I cried terribly. When the woman came out of the station crying, she fell into my arms and we cried together. I held her and we cried together. I barely had 20 dollar with me. But then a man who was walking by came to us and asked what was going on. I told him what had happened. This man, fortunately, had 50 dollar on him. He gave those to the woman, I added my 20 dollar and said to her ›You don't need to go to the police anymore, just drive directly to the hospital.‹«

There is no peace anymore…

»The conditions are getting worse and worse. Ten years ago, people were doing much better. And this year, 2019, is a completely different year. Everyone is frustrated because of the economic crisis. The situation is really bad[54]. Recently, I talked with a man whose four children come to my facility. This man used to have a good job in a household. Now he had lost this job. This was why he had come to me and cried. He is now unemployed. His wife is also staying at home. The two actually live in the North, but there is no work to be found there because the rain doesn't come anymore. All of their cattle died. It is as if today we are living in a different world. Everything has changed. The people are very desperate. There is no peace anymore.

Many – for example, the parents of the children that I take care of – do not have jobs. They do some domestic work, sell fatcakes or clean houses etc. They earn around 800 or 500 Namibia dollar a month. Some also help each other: You get 50 dollar and do laundry for me – something like that. But I can tell you, 90 per cent of all people here do not have a proper job. Men and women. They struggle to find work. Many sit at some corner and drink beer and simply have nothing to do.«

I tell them that they should not take their lives...

»For our settlement I can say that the number of people in need is growing day by day. Older women hear from other women that there is help to be found here. So, they come as well.

And you know that the families who we bring food to really are in need. The people come to me and plead for help. And I simply cannot ignore them. If I ignored them it would make me sick. They come to me; they put their lives in my hands. I try to be strong and deal with their problems. In December (when they come for the Christmas meal), I tell them that they should not take their lives. Because in December many people commit suicide. And I tell them not to abuse their children.«

---

54 The situation even worsened dramatically since the outbreak of the global CO-VID-19 pandemic.

The girl said: »It is true, I killed the baby...«

»In our settlement there is this girl, not even 15 years old – this girl had a child. And her mother: She's an alcoholic because of many problems. And the baby of the girl had no father. Probably, the man just got her pregnant and then abandoned her. Now the neighbours and other people in the area are talking about the girl. They say, for example: ›You are so young and have already been involved with men. And you have a child that is now fatherless.‹

This made the girl so desperate that one night she took her baby and went into the bush with it. There, she took a stone and smashed the baby's head with it. Then she half buried the baby. After that, she went home into her room and cried all day. When the others noticed this, they asked her: ›Where is your baby... where is your baby?‹ And she said: ›You people, you talked so much about this baby and that I had made a mistake, so I killed the baby.‹ And the people said: ›You cannot be serious?‹ The girl said: ›It is true, I killed the baby.‹ And she cried. So, the others went where the girl had told them she had buried the baby. There, they only found one leg of the baby. The rest had been eaten by the jackals. These are the kinds of stories of things that happen here.

Then there was, for example, a woman who went to a garbage dump. She had a baby and things were looking really bad for her. She couldn't breastfeed the baby anymore, because there was no milk in her breast. And she herself was starving. There was nothing left to eat at her house. She locked the baby up in her hut. Then she went to the garbage dump. Neighbours heard the crying baby in the hut and knocked on the door and shouted for the woman: ›Please, please you baby is crying a lot, where are you?‹ When the people saw that the house was locked and that they couldn't get in, they called the police. When the police arrived, they knocked against the door and the baby continued to cry. So, they thought: Maybe the mother is dead. They broke the door, entered, and found the baby [...] completely neglected and dehydrated. The child was hungry and close to dying. They took it with them and asked the neighbours about the mother. Those said they didn't know where the mother was. The child had cried incessantly. The police started to look for the mother. They used a megaphone through which they called for the mother by her name. When they finally came to the garbage dump, they found the mother sitting there and crying. The police officers took her into their car and asked her questions: ›Why did you lock up your baby?‹ She said: ›There is no hope for me, there is no help for me. I locked up the child because I did not want to see it starve and die. So I locked the child up in there and walked myself to the garbage dump so we could die at different places.‹ They took the woman and her baby to the hospital. I do not know what happened with the woman and the child after that. It was an event that even made its way to the newspapers.

You know, these people come from the north. And in the north, there is no hope. They come here in hopes of ›greener pastures‹. But here in the city there are no greener pastures and many women end up as prostitutes.

And what really frustrates me is that the birth control programme in hospitals is running out now because there is no more funding for it. There are no more supplies: no injections or other things to prevent pregnancies. Can you remember the girl with the injury on her eye? [...] She came here, I gave her money to go to the doctor. And you won't believe it, this young girl is getting involved with men. She is only 11 years old and goes to school here. But now she has stopped going to school. I called the social workers. But that didn't do anything. – It's like with the three orphans who lived with their blind grandmother who died and then left the three children all alone. I sat down with the authorities, laid out the issue, but nothing came of it.

So, this girl, she wanted money because her eye hurt, and she wanted to go to the hospital. I gave her 100 dollar. Some time later, she came back to me and thanked me. When adolescents come to me, I always help them as best as I can.

The children who used to come to my initiative and later started going to school, some of them still come to me after school. It seems that in some schools they've stopped the school meals. People say this stopped because there is no more money for it.«

I have a big dream...

»The children in my initiative: If I want to know what their situation at home is like, I let them draw pictures and ask them what it is they drew. In many cases it turns out that the children are beaten at home by their parents (or other adults). Abuse is also very frequent. The children are told: ›If you open your mouth and talk about this, I will kill you!‹ They are threatened. So, I give them paper if I want to know about the situation at their home. I tell the children: ›Anything you know, just draw it, draw it, draw it, draw it! Once you're done, you come to me and tell me what it is you drew.‹ And then the children explain: ›This here is dad, he hit mommy and mommy ran away.‹ And when they play you can also see what is happening at their homes and in their environment. And then, if you spot something unusual, you call the child and tell it: ›You know that I'm your teacher. You can trust me.‹ The children know that I love them, truly love them. I say to them: ›You can simply tell me. I am your friend. I'll send all of the others out of the room. Just you and me are here.‹ Or I talk with the children once everyone else has gone home. Then I say: ›Stay a bit, I'll bring you home but tell me, it's just the two of us now.‹ Then you'll see the child start to cry. And then it'll tell you what happened. Maybe that it is constantly being hit. If I find out something like that, I contact the parents. However, you cannot simply say to them: ›What are you doing to the child?!‹ You have to try to offer solutions to the parents. Only then can you get a good connection to them. And then you help where you can.

There was, for example, a little girl that had been raped by a bigger schoolboy. In that case, I couldn't simply go to the boy. I have to protect the children under my care. So what I did was call the mother and tell her about the situation and inform her as to where she can find help. I also gave her a couple of phone numbers of people who deal with cases like this. The mother then took care of the issue herself and the boy went into youth detention. Ultimately, it was found out that he had also raped other small girls.

Child drawing, March 2020. Hileni says to the children: »Draw whatever comes to your mind and then tell me what it is you drew.« Many children express their experiences with domestic violence in their drawings.

I have a big dream. I have a very big, big dream. I wish that these children have a chance to make something of themselves in the future. I don't want history to repeat itself again and again. You know, that they drop out after 7th grade, drop out after 4th grade, and then leave school. If I am old one day and have to walk with a stick I want to meet one of these kids again and hear: ›I became a doctor,‹ or, ›I am a professor‹, ›I am a teacher‹.«

Listening to Hileni, one could get the impression that Namibia, at least in Katutura, is a society on the verge of spinning out of control. There are a lot of figures on this – but just to name a few: According to statistics from 2018, in Namibia's urban centres 995,000 people (more than 40 per cent of the population) live in shacks made of corrugated-iron, wooden poles, cardboard, and tarpaulins. The average unemployment rate among people of working age is at 33,4 per cent. Around a third of the working population earns less than 1,000 Namibia dollar per month (which is approximately 67 USD). It is not uncommon for people to work 7 days a week.[55] The average monthly income of a day labourer in Windhoek is 2,500 Namibia dollar.[56] Approximately 80 per cent of the working population in Namibia earns less than 5,000 Namibia dollar per month.[57] The German-Namibian labour expert Herbert Jauch points out that the essential demand for minimum wages is problematic inasmuch as it could prompt companies that pay their employees well to from then onwards only pay the minimum wage.[58]

How is all of this possible? So many years after the independence in a country that is that rich in resources?

Namibia: a post-war society?

One can paint a dazzling picture of Namibia: Is Namibia a postcolonial society? The German colonial era lasted from 1884 until 1915. The era of Apartheid under political domination by South Africa lasted until 1990. One could say: For 106 years Namibia endured a colonial regime. A plethora of problems, which plague Namibia today can be seen as results of the de facto colonialism which lasted from the German colonial era until the end of Apartheid.[59]

---

55   The Namibian 2019.
56   Van Wyk 2019: 77.
57   The Namibian 2018b.
58   Ibid.
59   See also Melber 2015a/b and Wallace 2011.

Or is Namibia a post-war society? The liberation struggle which lasted from 1960 until 1989 and in which the People's Liberation Army of Namibia (PLAN), as a military branch of the South West African People's Organisation (SWAPO), fought against the South African occupying power, took many sacrifices until liberation was achieved. But it also inflicted deep, lasting wounds upon the Namibian society. Wound which until today have not healed, among other things because the SWAPO was very hard, even brutal, on suspected dissenters.[60] A reconciliation process like in the Republic of South Africa did not come to pass in Namibia. The SWAPO government, which at the time of independence started out with a rather socialist agenda, today is a government, which pursues neoliberal economics. It seems plausible to view this as an attempt to orient Namibia towards the model of a modern meritocracy.

What is going on in Namibia? Are what we see the scars of a postcolonial society? Do we see the wounds of a post-war society? Are we witness to the birth pangs of a modern meritocracy? Above all, it is the contrariness of the country, in which the White Apartheid rule only ended in 1990, that sticks out. Thriving tourism that can draw upon a string of the most beautiful places and cultivated lodges. A country whose future chances the World Bank assesses positively due to the richness in resources. A country with free press; a country where – which is exceptional for Southern Africa – there is a small old age pension; a country where vulnerable children have a right to modest social benefits. Also, a country in which elections, for the most parts, proceed free and unadulterated; a country with great ethnic diversity, where there are 13 official languages. And in spite of this diversity there are no manifest conflicts between ethnic groups. Currently, the president of the country is a member of the Damara, a group that occupies a rather marginal role in the country. The shopping malls in

---

60   Cf. The book by German pastor Siegfried Groth (1926–2011), former Africa correspondent of the Rhenish Missionary Society, which in 1989 uncovered the crimes of the SWAPO against dissidents: Groth 1996.

Windhoek offer everything that the global production has to offer: the bustle on the escalators, in the shops and supermarkets, the excessive building activity across the country, the daily traffic jams on the Independence Road in the middle of Windhoek – all of these paint the picture of a country that is awakening – a country that is on the path to becoming an African affluent society. Admittedly, Namibia's land is mostly deserts and semi-deserts. That said, the country possesses a wealth of mineral resources. Also worth mentioning is the small population of around 2,5 million people, the political stability, and the solid economic management – positive prerequisites which have, however, not led to the creation of new jobs or the reduction of the extreme socio-economic inequalities.[61]

Namibia is a divided country: Between the urban centre of Windhoek and the shanty towns of Katutura a mere handful of square kilometres separate worlds which could hardly be more different. A White (and by now also Black) elite and an emergent Black middle-class lead lives on a comparable standard to Europeans while the majority of the Black population lives in significantly more modest conditions.[62] Nearly 20 per cent of the population live in extreme poverty.[63]

A testament to this are the desperate deeds of young women and girls who abandon or kill their newborn children. The media reports about so-called »baby dumping« when a dead child is found in a dried-up riverbed or in the city sewers in the dunes on the coast. Or when a nearly suffocated child is dug up from beneath construction rubble or sometimes on a garbage dump. Those are the eruptions of the other Namibia.

---

61   Cf. the overview of Namibia on the website of the World Bank: https://www.worldbank.org/en/country/namibia/overview.

62   Overview of Namibia on the website of the German Federal Ministry for Economic Cooperation (BMZ): http://www.bmz.de/de/laender_regionen/subsahara/namibia/index.jsp.

63   New Era 2018.

The abandonments and killings of newborn children are increasing in frequency in Namibia, says a report from 2013.[64] The »Namibia Press Agency«, in January 2013, had claimed that in Windhoek a monthly average of 40 babies and foetuses were abandoned or flushed down the toilet. These figures were refuted as unproven. Meanwhile, the UNICEF report »Children and Adolescents in Namibia« from 2010 found that each month 13 dead babies were discovered in the sewage system of urban Windhoek.[65] Phil ya Nangoloh, the chairman of the National Society for Human Rights (NAMRIGHTS) in Windhoek, estimates that the actual number would be even higher if other Namibian cities were also considered. The reasons for baby dumping he sees in the de facto ban on abortion, which exists in Namibia; in poverty, in unemployment. Often pregnant girls are afraid of being kicked out of school and to fall into disgrace.

The withdrawal of many donor organisations, as a consequence of the World Bank's 2009 classification of Namibia as a middle-income country, has hit many civil society organisations as well as the welfare state hard.[66] But were there not a great many other African countries that needed help more urgently? Many Namibian NGO's which took care of vulnerable children and which were run with a mixture of voluntary work and paid jobs, which had already put them in continuous financial difficulties, had to cease their operations entirely – or limit them drastically. While this drew little public attention, it essentially worsened the situation of children over night. And all of this because the statistics that the World Bank uses for its categorisations paint a completely wrong picture: The statistics suggested that Namibia had become a country of middle-incomes. In reality, these statistics obfuscated the massive inequality in the country. Averaging the incomes created a wrong picture – which the World Bank was by no means unaware of.

---

64   VOA News 2013.

65   UNICEF 2010: 57.

66   The Southern Times 2016.

In addition to the high unemployment rate, there is the comparatively small number of people who graduate from an educational institution. Even for those who attain a degree have a hard time finding a job: In 2018, 67,000 graduated Namibians were unemployed.

This is the current situation in Namibia – and exacerbating this drastic Namibian inequality are the effects of climate change, which in 2019 brought a historic drought to Namibia. Climate change also affects farmers with big farms. In May 2019 we meet a vigorous farmer at the bar of a lodge, where he is serving wine and beer – because his farm can no longer sustain him. And climate change also and primarily impacts small subsistence farmers with a severity that puts their survival at risk. The effects are malnutrition and even hunger: The rural exodus is the obvious consequence. Currently, more than half of the 2,5 million population of Namibia live in rural areas, the majority of those in the former homeland, which was called Ovamboland and is situated in the Namibian north – now called the four O-regions (Oshana, Omusati, Oshikoto, Ohangwena).[67]

To comprehend the complex political situation in Namibia, one has to remember that the country is home to a multitude of ethnic groups: Ovambo, Nama, Damara, Herero, Kavango, Caprivians, Himba, Coloureds, Whites (mainly Boers and Germans). Aside from the indigenous languages and English, which serves as the official language, Afrikaans is widespread. Ethnic minorities feel disadvantaged by the Ovambo-dominated governing party, SWAPO, and accuse it of tribal politics – i.e. of serving primarily the interests of their own ethnic group. What Marc Augé anticipates for global society, albeit on a smaller scale, already apply to today's Namibia: »We are moving towards a three-classes world, divided into the powerful, the consumers, and the excluded.«[68] This book is about these latter, the excluded.

---

67   Namibia Statistics Agency 2017.

68   Augé 2019: 13.

The war generation and its children

The war is over. And at the same time, it is not. The liberation war that led to Namibia's independence ended 30 years ago. But essentially, nobody speaks about Namibian society as a post-war society – and that there are war memories which continue to be traumatizing for many up until today. Internal as well as external wounds remain. Ephraim is a Katutura resident who runs a bottle store with a bar. He is a comrade and a war veteran. And he is a dialysis patient. For a time, dialysis was paid for by the government. Now he has to pay for it himself. This, he cannot afford and so his days are numbered. One of his daughters, eleven-year-old Loide, has a heart defect. Since he has a renal disease and because the war memories weigh heavy on him, Loide wants to burden her father as little as possible with her own disease. This is why – as the girl tells it – she does not like talking about herself.

Again and again, one meets former participants of the war in Namibia, who now lament. However, aside from official memorial and victory celebrations, there continues to be no apparent historical reappraisal, no debate about long-term effects of the war that affect individuals.

The public silence about the war memories; the silence about consequences of war in the families. This silence is occasionally broken in the interviews and conversations because these memories are also and especially vivid in the memories of children of the war. Take Josef E. for example. Behind his corrugated-iron hut he has built a small oven in which he bakes the bread which he later sells. He remembers his childhood and youth in northern Namibia when – as he puts it – soldiers could appear at any moment and spread fear.

»As children, when we herded cattle and suddenly a military vehicle appeared, one of these big military vehicles, the cattle would bolt due to the noise. If you ran after the animals, soldiers would sometimes chase you. And then the animals would run onto the fields of other people and cause damage there. As children, we were really afraid in those situations: of the soldiers, but also of our own parents because the cattle had run over other people's fields. This was a very difficult time.«[69]

Josef's personal childhood memories about the sudden appearance of army vehicle tell the story of a childhood in the shadow of war, in a state of permanent fear. The official historiography speaks of the fights between the South African occupying forces and the soldiers of the SWAPO in northern Namibia as a protracted guerrilla war by the SWAPO.[70] A central event was the »Cassinga-Massacre«, May 4, 1978. There, the South African forces attacked a SWAPO base of operations in southern Angola and killed around 600 people. Among the victims were civilians and children. The SWAPO claims that this base which was bombed had been a refugee camp. The war finds many ways to cast its shadows onto the lives of the adults – but undoubtedly, also onto those of the children, many of whom were in fact the children of war children.[71]

A very striking form of expression was found in 2013 by then 17-year-old Mercia, a pupil from Katutura, who views Namibian society as a post-war society, one that is »morally exhausted«:

»Africans.
We are full of ›cans‹ filled with doubt.
We have mean ideas but no mental way out.
The past left a dent.
It happened to the parents but our youth is now also affected.
When will it take the youth to realize that it never happened before our eyes?
Everyday, over a million children go to school on empty stomachs.

---

69   Interview with Josef E., March 23, 2013, Katutura.

70   Cf. among others Wallace 2011.

71   In Germany, the situation of war children was only addressed extremely late (among others Bode 2014). Maybe the topic remains suppressed in Namibia?

These are the ones who have no choice.

It occurs because we have people in the parliaments earning salaries with endless zeros .

They spend their money on unnecessary projects to promote their image.

Our elders say that we have lost our morals and values, it's no longer within us.

Not knowing they depleted when they kept poisoning us with the constant encounters from the past.

Reading in the newspapers about fraud became a daily meal.

We were already fed by the lies of our leaders when we voted them into scene.

›Change, change, change,‹ this word has become such a cliche.

Our lands are so dry and open; we barely even have clean water; we scarcely have adequate food.

I'm mentioning the obvious but it's all just the truth.

I'm a scholar at Windhoek High School, does that make me better than everyone else? How can you be better when someone out there needs help?

We need people with integrity; people who speak what they do.

Men slaughtering our women because of patriarchy, women using our men because they were not properly raised by a ›king‹.

Nobody can tell the difference from wrong and right anymore; as long as it's beneficial – we're prepared to lose it all.

I won't sugar-coat anything, the truth must be heard.

Using the militia to end wars - It is like a pastor preaching to the congregation about leading by example; whilst raping a minor indoors.

It just doesn't correspond.

Africa in the eyes of its children - let the truth be uncovered.«[72]

---

72   Poem by Mercia N. from Windhoek (2013).

Transformations with catastrophic consequences

»For my part, I make a systematic defence of the non-European civ-
ilizations,« writes Aimé Césaire in 1950 in his blazing speech on the
crimes of colonialism.[73] A speech that not only speaks of crimes committed by colonialists but points to colonialism in general as a crime.
In 1950, at a time when colonialism was still in effect, Césaire counts
down several such crimes – for example: the denial of rights, police
use of truncheons, the labourers' protest which was quelled bloodily,
the punitive expeditions. »[...] every police van, every gendarme and
every militiaman, brings home to us the value of our old societies.«[74]
These precolonial African societies, which were racially discriminated
against and whose surviving remnants were then described as deficient and in need of modernisation, are characterised by Césaire in the
following words:

- »They were communal societies, never societies of the many for the
  few.
- They were societies that were not only ante-capitalist, as has been
  said, but also anti-capitalist.
- They were democratic societies, always.
- They were cooperative societies, fraternal societies.«[75]

»I make a systematic defence of the societies destroyed by imperialism,« Césaire writes.[76] Back then, this was a bold statement and even
upon repeating it today, one may earn incredulous amazement, head-
shaking, and ironic rejection. He does, however, not aim to advocate a
return to past forms of rural life but speaks of the path on which African societies had been when they were interrupted by colonialism.

---

73   Césaire 2000: 44.
74   Ibid.
75   Ibid.
76   Ibid.

Europe had expanded the moment it fell into the hands of the most unscrupulous finance and industry captains. And it had been Africa's misfortune to, on its path at the time, encounter this Europe and that this Europe »is responsible before the human community for the highest heap corpses in history«.[77]

Up until the present, people continue to discriminate against African ways of life and African approaches to economy by way of labelling them »backward«. This scandalous narrative is starting to topple only now as industrial civilisation is evidently outmanoeuvring itself. The industrial way of life has taken on massively self-destructive tendencies, so much so that its unquestioned dominance, which it used to discriminate African ways of life, is now waning. We will be witness to times in which African ways of life and economy will suddenly appear in an altogether different light. Perhaps they will finally be recognised as capable of survival compared to the industrial civilisation, while the latter continues to reveal more destructive facets day by day. Nobel prize laureate Amartya Sen had already in 1962 revealed that small-scale agriculture is far superior to large-scale farming in terms of harvest yield. Alas, this did not prevent propaganda from depicting smallholder farms as backward and act as if merging smaller enterprises were inevitable.[78]

The term »transformation« is popular in social sciences. It is steeped in the idea of progress and cannot deny its origins which lie in a history of disdain for the old, which is always associated with the static, the inflexible, the undeveloped. In step with how the self-destructive dimensions of industrial civilisation become more evident, the small voices from the remnants and ruins of old African ways of life might become more audible. In this, one also does have to expect the shrill voices of modernisers, which today resonate equally loudly

---

77   Ibid.: 45.

78   As such, the OECD demands that the fragmentation of land in Turkey be overcome in favour of larger units if the agrarian yield is to be increased. Cf. Monbiot 2008.

in big global organisations as among Black elites, who in case of doubt often personally benefit from radical agrarian modernisation, while definitely at least harbouring an unshakable sense of disdain for their own African past.

The small dissenting voices are audible to those who wish to listen to them. One shall be quoted here as an example. It almost magically attracts classical pejoratives: Especially ones like: »romanticising« and »culturally pessimistic«. Perhaps the impending crises of industrial civilisation will present us with a new chance to listen to the critics of this industrial civilisation - to Aimé Césaire, to Ivan Illich, Bruno Latour, to Charles Eisenstein. Eisenstein quote word from the shaman Davi Kopenawa, who is of the Yanomani people. The Yanomami live in the Amazon region, and their survival is – unsurpisingly – endangered.

> »The forest is alive. It can only die if the white people persist in destroying it. If they succeed, the rivers will disappear underground, the soil will crumble, the trees will shrivel up, and the stones will crack in the heat. The dried-up earth will become empty and silent. The xapiri spirits who come down from the mountains to play on their mirrors in the forest will escape far away. Their shaman fathers will no longer be able to call them and make them dance to protect us. They will be powerless to repel the epidemic fumes which devour us. They will no longer be able to hold back the evil beings who will turn the forest to chaos. We will die one after the other, the white people as well as us. All the shamans will finally perish. Then, if none of them survive to hold it up, the sky will fall.«[79]

An interesting, indigenous version of that which today is described under the label »transformation«. Davi Kopenawa and Bruce Albert in

---

79   Preface in Kopenawa/Albert 2013, quoted in Eisenstein 2019 (online edition, chapter »If we knew she could feel«: https://charleseisenstein.org/books/climate-a-new-story/eng/if-we-knew-she-could-feel).

their book »The Falling Sky: Words of a Yanomami Shaman« describe something which in the current mainstream automatically provokes defensive reactions: »apocalyptic!« or »pessimistic!« Today's official political discourse in fixated on the positive – if you do not play by this rule, you are out. Actually though, one cannot dismiss the possibility that the transformations which we are currently dealing with may take on apocalyptic streaks.[80]

That the sky comes crashing down is an impression one can get in today's Namibia. The 2019 drought – as already mentioned – had historic dimensions. Kopenawa's words had become reality, though in reverse: Nothing fell from thesky, not a single drop of rain for months. The groundwater level sank. Farmers in the South who used to find water 40 metres below the ground now have to dig 120 metres deep. In Kaokoveld tall grass used to sway high above the landscape after the rainy season. Today, hardly a blade of grass grows on the arid soil. In 2019, the drought forced commercial farmers to sell their cattle and many gave up on agriculture. Many smallholder farmer families who used to own bovine animals, sheep, or goats lost their livelihood to the drought. Many younger people, even children, moved to the cities and desperately searched for jobs and chances to survive.[81]

Corresponding to the crisis in Namibia is a crisis in the industrial nations. This latter one carries the danger that neo-colonial interventions wax while inhibitions against neo-colonial behaviour may wane.

»Nevertheless, the European habit of regarding African societies as being in need of expert advice to navigate the modern age remains pervasive. [...] Although no serious writer or politician today advocates the re-colonisation of Africa, items of colonial vocabulary and habits of thought that originated in colonial times continue to influence how

---

80   Cf. for example Hornschuh 2019.

81   Cf. for example the feature »Namibian capital city streets bursting with children as drought bites« of the press agency Xinhua: http://www.china.org.cn/world/Off_the_Wire/2019-05/20/content_74804601.htm.

Europeans, especially, think about Africa. In certain contexts, they even affect the way Africans think about themselves.«[82]

But maybe it is necessary to go beyond these sentences by Stephen El-lis and to radicalise them. Kathryn Yusoff is professor for »Inhuman Geography« at Queen Mary University of London. »I regard geology as a project that was racist from the outset,« she says. She speaks of »White geology«. White geology is an iteration of extractive cultures. Talk of the Anthropocene is arising now that White, liberal commu-nities suddenly feel threatened. The harm inflicted by extractive cul-tures in name of »civilisation«, »progress«, »modernisation« – was thus outsourced to Black and Brown cultures. The current narrative of the Anthropocene, which laments the impending »End of the World«, overlooks that imperialism and continuous (settler) colonialism in the past have always meant the end of the world for others. In this vein, Yusoff talks about a billion »Black Anthropocenes« – for Black people the end of the world has already happened.[83]

The thought comes to mind whether children in Namibia who are suffering, are victims of a destruction of traditional culture, which began with colonialism and is now being continued and perfected by consumerism that furthers the divide between the rich and the poor. Thus, the children of the marginalised become visible as victims. At the same time, we believe to have observed that victims are not mere victims but that they cope with the hardships of everyday life with re-markable fortitude. What does that mean? Maybe the phenomenon can be explained through the stories the children the tell?

If there is such a thing as »White geology« then there is probably also a »White sociology«. Will we succeed in this book to avoid what Yousoff calls »deliberate blindness«, which consists of perpetuating

---

82   Ellis 2011: 17.

83   Yusoff 2018: XI-XIV.

the comfortable assumptions and notions of our planet which they –
i.e. White geology and White sociology – hold?[84]

Orphans and vulnerable children: the experiences of children

Justina Vatilange Matatias is a young woman from Swakopmund who
in 2013 participated in an essay contest, which was announced in the
country's most important press medium, the »Namibian«. For its im-
pressive and vivid description of her situation in life, the essay won the
first prize as best contribution in the contest. Justina was 15 years old
when she wrote the essay, almost still a child. She writes:

> »In life, I realised something. I realised that care is very important for
> everyone. Let me share my true story with the youth of Namibia. I'm
> a 15-year-old girl doing Grade 8 in Swakopmund in the Erongo Region.
> I grew up with my aunt. I learnt a lot in life. I came with her to Swa-
> kop in 2004, starting school in 2005 Grade 1 at Festus Gonteb Junior
> Primary School. Living with her, I went through thick and thin, but
> I'm still strong and standing. I grew up far away from my biologi-
> cal parents and didn't receive any care or love from them, I grew up
> like an orphan. My aunt treated me so badly that I even wanted to
> take my own life. She promised my parents to take care of me and
> treat me as if I was her daughter, but she didn't fulfil her promise.
> However, she secured a place in a school for me, which I'm very gra-
> teful for. My mother is an Angolan, while my father is from Namibia.
> When they separated from each other, my mother went back to her
> country in 2007 and that was the last time I saw her. I only came to
> meet her in August this year, when I went the extra mile to go look for
> her in Angola. I never visited her while she was in Namibia, because
> I was treated like a slave. My aunt didn't like it when I visited my mo-

---

84   Ibid.: XIII.

ther. I cried day and night. I always prayed, but God, it seems that God did not hear my prayers. Finally God answered my prayers. I moved out of my aunt's house and I am now living with good Samaritans. At the moment these good Samaritans are taking care of me with assistance from my father. They treat me like their biological child, maybe because God didn't bless them with kids. I'm like their only biological kid now. I believe that whether your parents are alive or not, it won't make any difference unless you are living with them. All you need to do as an individual is be self-confident and have high self-esteem. I believed that with God everything is possible. Talking from my own experience, I suffered like an orphan, but my parents are still alive. I used to do all the chores and go to school with an empty stomach. I was like a nanny, but still that didn't affect my school work, I'm just as smart as a star. It's very hard to grow up far away from your parents, especially if they are alive. We know in our country people are dying of HIV/AIDS. The number of orphans every day is just skyrocketing. It's very painful, when you lost your parents, because of HIV/AIDS. Unfortunately there is nothing we can do about that, we just need to take care of the orphans and of course let's not forget to educate the nation about the HIV/AIDS pandemic. As a result of people dying of HIV/AIDS leaving their innocent children behind, there will be no one to take care of them. These children might drop out of school, become criminals, start sleeping around with sugar daddies/mummies to get money, end up being pregnant and infected with the deadly disease. These are things that are happening around us, in communities and we are doing nothing about these. I urge the government to take care of orphans and street kids, to make sure that they are protected and safe. Despite all this, my message to the youth is for them to be strong and follow their dreams. We all can do it, we are the future leaders!«[85]

85   »I grew up like an orphan«, in: Fink/Gronemeyer (2013): 105 et seq. as well as: The Namibian 2013.

The experiences that this Namibian girl has had spared nothing and she directly addresses that which to many Namibian children sums up their experiences: separation, loss, childhood with a loveless surrogate mother, hunger, abuse, and exploitation (»slave labour«). It is a biography from outside of the suffocating consumerist reality to which many European children are exposed. A biography as stern, austere, and as clear as the image of a prophet at the portal of a Romanesque church. No cliché, no kitsch. »I cried day and night.« The girl lists facts that nobody can argue with. And yet: no cheap surges of emotion, no whining to demand sympathy, but the designation of sheer plight. Fierce and strong is what these sentences are. She had been close to suicide. She tells this like it is a side note. And one believes her. »I am just as smart as a star.« One can almost envision the clenched fist. And these words come from someone who is standing atop the ruins of their childhood. Actually, perhaps only someone standing atop the ruins of their childhood can say these words in this way. The unadorned statement of facts is (much to the amazement of us who are used to secularisation) in line with a religiousness which does not exist in rhetorical phrases but which arises from intense religious experiences: She speaks of prayers that go unheard. Of prayers which finally, as she sees it, bring change to her situation in life. And thus, it comes to pass that she ends up with people who she calls Samaritans; people who treat her as if she were their own child. It is she who finally travels to Angola to seek out her mother. She almost tells it ironically: »I went the extra mile,« to find a mother who had not cared for her. And her words are far from any narcissistic yammering. At the end, she does not talk about herself but about the state and the youth. She demands that the government of the country take care so that the children of Namibia may have something to eat each day. And of the youth which she is part of she demands that they be strong and follow their dreams. This speech, which she writes there, the speech that her essay leads to, does not bespeak a desire to have something but a dream future in which apathy is pushed aside and which is characterised by strong political will. A speech that one could imagine being held in an Athenian polis: It is focused on the essential, necessary things in life. One could also say: on the *conditio humana* – the basic human condition.

The situation of orphans and vulnerable children has been the subject of several studies. Kristen Cheney found out that »childhood vulnerability« causes ambivalent reactions. In short, Cheney claims that scientific and humanitarian activities may not necessarily decrease vulnerability but possibly increase it.[86] This repeats something, which already became apparent in the discussion on the global validity of human rights: global humanitarian ideologies differ from local ways of describing vulnerability, of comprehending and treating it. The international donor scene is often pervaded with a neoliberal philosophy that views deregulation and privatisation as panacea to lay the foundation for economic growth. This, Cheney argues, is a dangerous illusion.[87] As a consequence, increasingly radical ways are used to construct children as »victims« in need of saving. Evangelical organisations working in the domain of vulnerable children display particularly close ties to the ideology of free markets. More expansive definitions artificially increase the number of orphans and vulnerable children, which diverts attention away from questions as to what causes poverty and structural violence. Children are thus turned into addressees of interventions by the humanitarian industry, which is upheld by neo-conversative and evangelical movements.

Another important aspect was contributed to the discourse by Helen Meintjes and Sonja Giese.[88] The global attention that the topic of AIDS orphans has drawn reinforces stereotypes about the experiences of affected children while also changing local perceptions and local ways of dealing with the issue. In a 2006 article, the authors analyse official statistics which imply a dramatical situation. In 2003, UNICEF reported more than 34 million orphans in sub-Saharan Africa, 11 million of which had been orphaned by AIDS. Meintjes and Giese

---

86   Cf. Cheney 2010 and Cheney 2017.
87   Cf. in particular Ferguson 2006.
88   Meintjes/Giese 2006: 407–430.

point out that for the vast majority of these estimated orphans it can be assumed that they still have one living parent.[89] Furthermore, they argue that the category »orphan« is not necessarily meaningful: Children with two living parents who are both unemployed could live in much poorer conditions than children whose parents died but who live with relatives. Also, the global term orphan often does not correspond at all to local perceptions. »Are my children orphans because their father died?« asks a mother who finds it offending when people label her children as orphans. Nurses at a clinic near Cape Town say: An orphan is a child who no one takes care of. If a child is in the care of its grandmother, then it is not an orphan. Even if someone has lost both parents – if somebody takes care of them, they are not viewed as orphans. In short: There is a wide gap between the globally widespread image and local experiences and ways of dealing with it. International definitions, which are based on biological orphanhood pay too little attention to social dimensions. But because the »orphan« status can be beneficial with regards to international interventions some children are labelled orphans or they refer to themselves as orphans to reap the benefits, although they are in the care of their grandmothers or someone else.[90]

Excursus: children's rights

>»White people think of themselves as white and without a race, just as men (and often women) consider gender to be an issue for women. The claim of unsituatedness is made by and on behalf of those with power. To the extent the Convention [on the Rights of the Child] deals with children as unspecified, unsituated people, it tends in fact to deal with white, male, and relatively privileged children.«[91]

---

89   Ibid.: 410 et seq.

90   Ibid.: 422, 425; also cf.: Fink/Gronemeyer 2015.

91   Olsen 1995: 195, quoted in: Liebel 2019: 21 (and Liebel 2020: 127).

This observation by author Frances Olsen (quoted in Manfred Liebel) is undeniably true. The children who we talk about in this book are therefore described in their social situations – in rural and in urban areas. However, the postcolonial dilemma remains. And it is this post-colonial dilemma which Manfred Liebel speaks of. What is it? When we describe the situation of vulnerable children, do we use the situation of well-situated European children as the comparative standard? How should their situation change? Is the explicit or unspoken goal against which we measure the situation of Namibian children that of European middle class? This does not make sense for two reasons: First, a living standard like this is (currently) unattainable for the children we talk about here. Second, it is becoming more and more questionable whether the imitation of that lifestyle is desirable in the first place. Postcolonial theories reinforce these doubts: The supposed superiority of European modernity is questionable, and its role model status becomes increasingly unstable. Children's rights as they exist today obviously hail from Western origins and the Western influence in them is undeniable. If one unceremoniously takes them as the standard and applies them to the situation of children in the global South, a whole set of questions arises.[92] According to postcolonial theory, this approach is currently perpetuating racist devaluation and discrimination.[93] This is why children's rights must be de-centred – with regard to the situation of children in postcolonial regions, they have to be reconceptualised.[94] Children's rights should be »usable from the bottom«, or they should be relativised by assigning them to the »Province Europa«.[95] The UN Convention on the Rights of Children (passed in 1989) can certainly be considered as a step forward inasmuch as it, for the first time, recognised children as legal subjects. That being said, the Convention leaves

---

92   Liebel 2019: 22.

93   Ibid.: 22 et seqq.

94   Ibid.: 24 (regarding different studies).

95   According to Liebel 2019: 24 (referring to Gayatri Spivak and Dipesh Chakrabarty) (own translation of the quote).

little room for viewing children in anything but the structural pattern of modern »Western« childhood.

Children's rights are in a difficult conflicted area between cultural relativism and universal human rights. Both approaches can be abused in racist ways, both can be used to improve the situation of marginalised children. Manfred Liebel writes:

> »Just as the critique of Eurocentric tendencies in the discourse on human rights and their application is justified and necessary, one also has to consider the risks of overemphasising cultural relativist arguments. Children, being social subjects whose perspectives are often treated as of little value, are particularly vulnerable when universalism and cultural relativism are dogmatically understood and practised.«[96]

One of the consequences of the criticism levelled against Eurocentrism in the Convention on Children's Rights is the development of an African charta on children's rights, which some African governments have attempted. Central to this: For the first time, in addition to the protection of human rights the duties shall be expressed, which individuals have towards their country and other legally recognised communities. This includes the duties of children (for example in the family) and calls for children to show solidarity and help each other. Traditions in this process are no longer dismissed as backwards. Instead, the contribution of local traditions is recognised.[97]

Vanessa Pupavac adds another aspect to these insights which is particularly important for our context: The anchoring of children's rights is clearly distinct from its previous model which Pupavac calls the »moralising child-salvation model«.[98] Furthermore, she argues that the institutionalisation of children's rights takes place during a time of severe moral, political, and social crises. The tremors that pass

---

96   Ibid.: 40 (own translation of the quote).
97   Recknagel 2010: 77.
98   Pupavac 2001: 96.

through traditional institutions and sources of authority coupled with the absence of other universal integrative myths leads to children being elevated to integrative symbols of society.[99] In the global South with its young population just as in the global North, the child becomes the last remaining source of an irrevocable, immutable primary relation.[100] The institutionalisation of children's rights (Pupavac calls it the »International Children's Rights Regime«) suggests that there is a universally applicable model for development during childhood which is connected with likewise universal needs.[101] This generates an action model in which colonial patterns are repeated: The grown-up North offers aid to the infant South, with the effect that governmental and non-governmental actors in the West gain power by appearing as moral actors in favour of children in the South.[102]

Pupavac points out another aspect that reinforces the dominance of Western perspectives: The fear that children who, for example, experience violence through war could turn violent themselves: »Inter-governmental and non-governmental agencies have all adopted the cycle of violence thesis and its assumption that children exposed to violence or trauma do not have the same capacity for moral development.«[103] The author opens up a very critical view on the interventions of Western »therapeutic cultures«. These carry the risk that international West-oriented experts propagate educational practices, which are not capable of preparing children to cope with the difficult realities, which they may have to face in their respective societies. In aid programmes, the priorities of donor countries are given more consideration than those of the society in which a child lives. Missionaries of the 19th century, Vanessa Pupavac elaborates, spoke of the necessity to bring civilisation to the indigenous while today's human rights campaigns operate under the question how to support children's

---

99   Ibid.: 97.

100   Beck 1994: 118.

101   Cf. Gronemeyer 2002.

102   Pupavac 2001: 103.

103   Ibid.: 104.

rights and how to create a tolerant culture. This, however, implies the assumption that the education styles of people in the non-Western world, i.e. their cultural practices, are the problem. This is why international organisations assume that external specialists are needed to define uniform social norms and see to their global institutionalisation.[104] Brazilian educationalist and liberation theologian Paulo Friere already criticised this paternalistic attitude in the seventies and coined the term »the director societies« in reference to the demonisation of non-Western societies.[105]

Pupavac speaks of a return of the topos of »White man's burden«, originally formulated by Rudyard Kipling in 1898: In the South, people live who are half devil and half child. At least the 19th century missionaries had assumed that these people could be saved and progress brought to them. The Children's Rights Regime, on the other hand, at its core and in regard to human relations is misanthropic and characterised by a deterministic model of child development and human behaviour. »The children's rights regime effectively denies the emotional, moral and political capacity of children and adults alike, leading to a propensity to demand ever greater regulation both domestically and internationally.«[106]

The debate around children's rights and the Convention on Children's Rights shows how many paternalistic and postcolonial dangers are hidden within the topic of childhood. The core thesis of this book emphasises the genuine competence of children and speaks of their sovereignty and fortitude, yet it does not hide the difficult life situation of children.

---

104   Ibid.: 109.

105   This was pointed out by Pupavac: loc. cit.: 109.

106   Pupavac 2001: 109. Also cf. Esetva 1993 and Illich 2003; Helen Penn analyses the perspective of the World Bank on early childhood and how much this perspective is characterised by Anglo-American notions of family, community, and childhood – as well as how this perspective is used to justify interventions in so-called developing countries. See Penn 2002.

II. Children in Rural Areas

Egumbo: The situation of children in rural areas

The rural Namibian north is a culturally rich and agriculturally rather special region. During the German colonial times, it was nominally
claimed as sovereign territory of the German government, while in
reality their area of influence ended around the edge of the Etosha
pan. Fort Namutoni, which today lies within the area of the Etoscha
National Park, was the outermost outpost of the German colonial government. Anything north of that was what was then called the »Police
Zone«. The 1963 Odendaal Plan (the counterpart to the Homeland policy of the South African Union) proposed the creation of homelands in
South West Africa (today's Namibia). The Ovambo were to be resettled
to a region called Ovamboland in the north of Namibia, an area, which
today is administratively divided into Ohangwena, Omusati, Oshana,
and Oshikoto.[107]

To date, the landscape is primarily characterised by two elements
which, in a sense, serve as pillars of the traditional rural existence
in northern Namibia: the ponds (the *lishana*, singular: *oshana*) which
emerge during rainy season and the landscape's characteristic ensem-
ble of huts and fields (the *omagumbo*, singular: *egumbo*).

Before we describe these pillars, it has to be mentioned right away
that these pillars are crumbling, even breaking down. It is no exagger-
ation to claim that the cultural and agrarian richness of this countryside in north Namibia, its diversity and beauty, are as threatened as

---

107 See among others Wallace 2011 and Tönnies 1911.

the rain forests of the Amazon. However, while the disappearance of
the rain forests at least attracts worldwide attention, the cultural rain
forest of north Namibia disappears silently, unnoticed, and definitive-
ly. This destruction of a differentiated ancient culture does not even
merit a shrug by the relevant institutions. Neither the Namibian government nor the UNESCO, which bestows upon sites, according to their
uniqueness, authenticity, and integrity, a status as World Cultural or
Natural Heritage. And world heritage is what this former Ovamboland
is to anyone with ears and eyes for the beauty of this silent bush landscape. This landscape fills all senses with the scent of wild herbs, the
humane moderation in settlements, its glittering blue lakes, its fires
and huts. The destruction, meanwhile, works in two ways: Migration
undermines the ancient lifeworld from within. Men in particular leave
the area, the HIV/AIDS epidemic has compounded the issue. At the
same time, an aggressive modernity cleaves asphalt aisles into the regions; aisles to which concrete deserts cling, where banks, malls, gas
stations, government buildings, hospitals, or universities proclaim
their dominion over the present and past of the landscape. A crass side
by side of fading subsistence lifeworld and unfettered bureaucratic
consumerism. Between the two, the victor has already been decided.
The desolation of the countryside and of peasant culture go hand in
hand.

The first pillar of the traditional agrarian lifeworld are the *lishana*. In
places where the landscape of northern Namibia is slightly hilly, the
dried-up ponds, the lishana, fill up with rainwater during rainy season
(between October and March). Fish and frogs who waited out the dry
season during beneath the ground become easy prey for adolescents
who catch them and dry them in the sun. But this water also serves as
potable water, water for cooking and for laundry. Presumably, in earlier times there were at least partial systematic connections between the

lishana through trenches and small canals.[108] Driving through the bush, one occasionally catches a glimpse through the foliage and spot what looks like a green or blue laguna, surrounded by reeds, framed with fine sand. The many animals that used to roam these lands, including leopards, lions, and giraffes, have disappeared. Cows and goats now populate the bush. And from time to time one can see a young pastoralist, supporting themselves on their staff, plastic bottle in hand, close to their herd. Some still carry a few arrows and a bow, which they use to hunt the remaining small animals. Back in the day, herders used to spend many weeks in the bush and thus had to hunt game to sustain themselves. This has changed, in part also because compulsory education, which, admittedly, some families do not heed, does not allow for such long absences. But young people used to know a lot about bushes and trees whose fruits are edible; about roots that are worth digging up; about plants with healing properties.[109] This knowledge still exists among the elderly but most of the young people have lost it. Survival in the bush? The knowledge is not needed any more. After all,

---

108 Today it is no longer recognisable that up until the 19th century people handled the water with foresight and subtlety. For example, pools were created and interconnected. Impressed, the traveler Gerald McKierman wrote in 1876: »In the settled portions of the country the natives make immense excavations in the omarambas (flood channels) which fill in the rains and serve through the dry season for man and beast.« Quoted in: Kreike 2004: 18seqq. See also the research of Martin Zimmermann on traditional techniques of water supply in Ovamboland: »The area of investigation is the so-called Cuvelai-Etosha-Basin which is located in central northern Namibia. It is estimated that 1 million people live in this area, which is approximately half of the Namibian population. There are no perennial rivers within the region and groundwaters are saline. To supply the population with potable water, a large technical system has been established which is fed by the Namibian-Angolan border river Kunene. However, at the same time, traditional water supply techniques such as Oshanas and excavation dams (Ometale), shallow dug wells (Omuthima), dug wells (Oshikweyo), and rainwater harvesting play a considerable role.« Zimmermann 2010 (quoted from the abstract of the article: https://namibian-studies.com/index.php/JNS/article/view/73).

109 On Namibia's traditional medicinal plants see e.g. van Koenen 2008.

there is something absurd to young Ovambos disappearing into the bush while not 20 kilometres away, in Oshakati for example, self-service hamburger shops line the sides of an asphalt road. Shoprite, the South African supermarket chain, offers convenience food (already prepared salad, for example, nicely packaged in plastic), meanwhile a couple kilometres away millet porridge is cooked just like in the old times. This perplexing juxtaposition is also reflected in the fact that 50 Namibia dollar (approximately three to four USD) get you nowhere in the supermarket, while the same 50 dollar are a decent amount of money in the bush: Essentially, it is two currencies, which derive their value depending on whether they are grasped by an electronic cash till in a supermarket or the wrinkly hands of an old woman in the *egumbo*.

Which brings us to the social heart of northern Namibia. To the *egumbo*. This is what the Ndonga call the cluster of huts in which they traditionally live and keep house. The Kwanyama call it *eumbo*. The Ovambo language has several dialects, which correspond to the different ethnic groups. There are an estimated 1.6 million Ovambo,[110] most of whom live in the north of Namibia while a small minority can be found in southern Angola. They are the largest ethnic group in Namibia and the (former) Ovamboland is the most densely populated area in the country. Nearly half of the population lives here.[111]

The *egumbo* consists of a circular palisade, which encloses several round huts. These are built from stakes that are covered in clay, and their roofs are made from straw or grass.[112]

The palisades (unlike in the old times) can no longer be made from mopane trees – this was forbidden by the government. Here and there, stones, corrugated iron, and barbed wire can be found as replacements.

---

110 Tonchi et al. 2012: 330–331.
111 See the online information at https://www.info-namibia.com/regions/north-central.
112 Traditionally, the roof is made of dried grass or millet stems. Cf. Erkkilä/Indongo 2017: 230; the Botswanian *lolwapa* is for the most part the equivalent of the *egumbo*. Cf. Larsson 1996.

The huts in egumbo serve different purposes and are divided into social spheres through plaited fences: an area for boys (which is traditionally located located next to the entrance for protection against intruders); an area for girls, the reception area for the man (*oshoto*), the kitchen hut, the huts of women, the hen hut, and – especially important: *omashisha*, the large plaited containers in which harvested millet is stored, safe from vermin and moisture. These millet containers are what guarantees survival until the next harvest and in that sense represent a sort of secret centre of the *egumbo*. A kraal for cows or goats might be part of it – in any event, the area around the *egumbo* is dedicated to millet fields, which during harvest season almost completely conceal the *egumbo*. *Mahangu* is foxtail millet, the staple food in the region. Between the millet, beans, spinach, and pumpkins are planted. Spinach was and is shaped into small flat cakes and dried in the sun on a rooftop. Trees which carry edible fruits are also part of the farmstead: Towards the end of the rainy season in April, embe, small, hazelnut-sized fruits, are plucked from the omive tree in large quantities. The fruits of the *marula tree* are particularly important. The *marula* fruit is about the size of a walnut, its cores can be processed into oil while their pulp can be turned into a very popular sour, lightly alcoholic beverage.

The *egumbo* has two entrances. An official one for visitors who stand in front it and call »*erapo*« to ask for permission to enter. The answer is an elongated »*aeaeaeeeh*«. The guest then asks: »*ongini?*« Response: »*nawa aeh aeaeaeaehh*«. And thus begins the long constantly repeating series of greetings in which people enquire about each other's well-being, night rest, daily affairs, and family. Later, when everyone is sitting on the floor or a tree stump inside of the *egumbo*, the greetings are sometimes begun anew, only this time people do not look at each other but rather repeat the greetings to themselves in whispers. The back entrance leads to the place of the chicken, to the small vegetable garden, and the goat shed. Among wealthier people, the front entrance is sometimes expanded into almost a maze of mopane stakes and leads into the inner egumbo through winding paths. Among the traditional authorities of the Kwanyama and Ndonga, who they refer to as king and queen, this results in a long, pleasant rapprochements until one reaches the inside. There, one enters the reception area for the man (*oshoto*) where tree trunks are arranged in a U-shape. The mopane stakes are adorned with the horns of mighty bulls. In this area, which is open to the sky above, the man's body will one day be laid out, across from the bull skulls, which serve as reminders to his ancestors and to his own life.

Traditionally, young men guarded the entrance to the egumbo and because of that, they inhabited the huts next to it. The sections are divided by wooden plaited fences, which enables a refined mixture of potential distance and control. One can hear if anything forbidden happens; one can hear if the girls return in time, but one cannot see them.

After a couple of years, there may be a decision to move the entire egumbo a few hundred metres away. This is a lot of work and is most likely done in the event that fields are exhausted and rotation therefore necessary.[113]

In the *egumbo* one traditionally finds a lot of devices and containers that are crafted by the inhabitants: plaited bowls, carved wooden mugs, clay pots, hoes, etc. A farmstead like this is located far away from the next of its kind – sometimes within shouting distance, sometimes at a greater distance. Traditionally, land here is not in short supply. It is communal land, which is assigned by the traditional authorities. Currently, this tradition is destroyed as large swathes of land are illegally fenced in with barbed wired.[114]

These days, more and more members of the new elite move to the communal land. Instead of the landless, dispossessed population, they often benefit from the government's resettlement programme. They build modern houses, use the property often just as a vacation home, accelerate privatisation of the communal lands – i.e. changes in the land law so that the land can become official property. The land-

---

113   Cf. Erkkilä 2017.
114   Cf. Odendaal/Hazam 2018.

ed properties of the elite in many cases are unproductive inasmuch as
they do not contribute to the production of foodstuff.

Not only the crafted items and gestures characterise the egumbo
but also the chanting, dancing, the tales, the knowledge about disease and healing, about the rhythms of life, about birth and death.
The egumbo traditionally is a small microcosm onto itself where strict
rules determine education, nutrition, the ways of dealing with birth
and death, maturity and sexuality, as well the relationships between
men and women or the young and the elderly. Who ploughs the fields,
who sows, who weeds, who harvests, who threshes, who grinds the
millet, who cooks, who herds the cattle, who fetches water, who tends
to the fire, who maintains the huts and harvest containers – all of this
has been arranged for generations. Whenever the rain failed to fall and
a famine threatened the area, the king and queen were obligated to
distribute the dues that had been collected in better seasons among
the people. And when misfortune befell someone and they did not have
millet or seeds, the neighbours would fill discreetly placed baskets

*Egumbo (Oshindonga)/Eumbo (Oshikwanyama): the traditional farmstead
of the Ovambo*

Oshoto (Oshindonga) / Olupale (Oshikwanyama): the man's reception area

Eshisha (Oshindonga) / Okaanda (Oshikwanyama): the millet silo

Oshini (Oshindonga/Oshikwanyama): the place where millet is mashed into flour.

Elugo (Oshindonga) / Epata (Oshikwanyama): the cooking place

with millet which would help the person in need to survive and sow anew. This ancient gesture is still practised here and there today.[115]

The old *egumbo* was made from materials that could be found on the ground and the surrounding area. They cost nothing but time and effort. Often, neighbours would help with the construction and upon finishing a building they would celebrate with millet beer. The *egumbo* offered protection for the extended family and a place were everyone had a task to fulfil. The nutritional diet was varied and rich if rain fell and the inhabitants took care of ploughing, sowing, weeding, and harvesting.

One could well argue that the *egumbo* was (and in part still is) the essence of subsistence life. A way of life which, by the way, used to exist in this or a similar form of farmstead living across the world. Ivan Illich writes the following sentences, which could fully apply to the *egumbo* as well, about Mahatma Ghandi's hut:

>This house is made of wood and mud. In it's making, it is not the machine, but the hands of man which have worked. I call it a hut, but it is really a home. A house is where man keeps his luggage and furniture. It is meant for the security and convenience of the furniture than of the man himself.«[116]

No farmstead home – including the *egumbo* – is every really finished. It grows and changes with its inhabitants, but today it is discredited as a shelter and home: It is regarded as old-fashioned, primitive, and poor.

The *egumbo* is a way of life that allows people to inscribe their life trails upon the landscape. It is neighbourly architecture, just as unique as neighbourly language, which had its own colourations and varieties from place to place. The structural grammar of the *egumbo* is at best similar in the former Ovamboland but no two *omagumbo* are identi-

---

115 Cf. Dohr/Kumria/Metzger 2015.

116 Illich 1992: 66 (see also the online article on the website: https://www.mkgandhi.org/museum/msgofbapuhut.htm).

cal. People have the means to repair it themselves, it can be mended, expanded, tailored to new wishes. It is not patriarchal architecture since women and men have to cooperate to build it. The serial rooms, which are built within the national housing construction programmes, force people into debt. They are not variable. They cement family relations: They have relinquished the genuine in favour of convenience and standardisation. In the serial room ethnic traditions vanish, different languages disappear and are replaced by Namish, a Namibian variety of English that tastes of plastic and globalisation. The contemporary consumer of living space lives in a different world than the inhabitant of the egumbo. One can, for example, find this new inhabitant in the serial houses, in apartment flats, in single-family homes in Ongwediva, the burgeoning area between Ondangwa and Oshakati. City folk have left rural life behind themselves and expertly handle the new devices, adopted the new gestures: the steering wheel of the pickup, the smartphone, the flatscreen, the current account, the freezer.

»The building is constructed from the point of view of these conveniences. It is made of cement and bricks and it is like a box where the furniture and other conveniences can fit in well«, remarks again Illich.[117]

The *egumbo* used to be a reflection of the cosmos. It is now becoming a reflection of the contemporary catastrophe that is dissolving the old social milieus – without putting new reliable patterns or milieus in its place.

The *egumbo* is falling apart. It has become an area of women who, together with their children, try to survive. The men, for the most part, have disappeared: to the diamond mines of Oranjemund, to the fish factories of Walvis Bay, to the wage labour of Windhoek or Swakopmund; they are labourers on distant farms or in lodges or just in the cuca shop next door where beer is poured.

Egumbo used to be not just an assemblage of huts but also the term for the (extended) family. It too is becoming void with the collapse of

---

117 Ibid.

the egumbo as a social arrangement. Among other things, the HIV/
AIDS epidemic has severely damaged this social and life form.

The *egumbo* used to be a place of agrarian subsistence life; a place
where men, women, and children were involved in a clear division of
labour, integrated into a rich network of social rules, of behavioural
expectations, and a life rhythm, which comprehends people's biog-
raphies in parallel and conjunction with the changing seasons. Men
plough, women sow and harvest. Boys herd the cattle, girls fetch and
boil water. *Efundula*, the maturity celebration of girls, marked their en-
try into the life of a woman – and there were heavy punishments if a
girl got pregnant before the *efundula*. There was a patriarchal order to
things: At the *oshoto*, the reception area of the man, who was allowed
to have multiple wives if he could provide for them, the bleached skulls
and horns of bulls symbolised the power and strength of the man.

Today, now that the men have disappeared, something becomes apparent which may have always been true: that the women, in secret or
overtly, actually ruled because they guarded the food, the children, the
tools, and the huts; perhaps not because they ruled but – as one would
classically put it – maintained control over production goods. Today, the
Namibian north is a region in which women primarily keep shop on their
own and confidently try to master their modest, meagre lives.

»Reality lies in the small things,« said author Botho Strauß[118]: A
sentence which the inhabitants of the *egumbo* do not know, but which
they have been living by for a long time. Someone who grew up there
describes the loss:

> »They people were exposed to Western culture and wanted to be free
> and to say: We are a democracy now. And because of that they do
> not follow the rules of their parents. In our tradition, it is unusual for
> someone below the age of 18 to go out and come back past 10 in the
> evening. If you go out at six, you have to ask permission and let people
> know where you are going. In the remote rural areas, it is still done this

---

118   Strauß 1984: 114 (own translation of the quote).

way. It is not allowed to simply go out with boys and girls. If there is a festival, you only go with your parents' permission, and if the parents are also there, they make sure that you go home with them. If you get closer to the cities, these basic rules do not apply anymore. Girls and boys often sleep somewhere else and do not return home for days at a time. [...] Until they had reached a certain age, girls used sleep with their mothers, they boys sometimes with their fathers. And so, there was always a level of control and the father knew that you were close.

The closer you get to the city, the less control there is. The men venture to the south to find work. The women remain. Recently, women have also occasionally started to venture to the south. Those men who go south but do not find a job there stay there and sometimes turn into criminals and all of that [...]«

This is how Titus M., principal of a vocational school in northern Namibia, put it in the year 2000.[119] Titus M. comes from a rural area himself and laments that people back at home do not understand him anymore.

Well, this can be read as a familiar story: The »good old times« have passed and there is no bringing them back. The suspicion of romanticism seems reasonable. One immediately feels the need to clarify that one does not want to turn back the wheel of time. This, however, does not make the question go away as to what steps in to replace the former and which cultural treasures crumble in the process. The transition from the limited rural lifeworld of the *egumbo* to the modern urban world, which in northern Namibia happens across a stretch of a few kilometres, moves children from a cosmos of modesty to a new world where everything is different, in which (nearly) everything is purchasable. Here, wares are enticingly dangled in front of you, which most cannot afford, but which nonetheless create the gnawing feel-

---

119 Interview with Titus M., October 14, 2000, Ondangwa, northern Namibia. Quoted in Gronemeyer 2002: 98 et seq.

ing that something is being denied to you, which you could have. All of a sudden, the consumerist promises are there, they presuppose the possession of money, which most people do not have. What used to be the agrarian modest cosmos of the egumbo has become a glitteringly attractive witch's cauldron: You can feel it if you go to the Shoprite parking lot in Odangwa: Incredibly loud music is blaring from a store that sells t-shirts and sports shoes; have-nots push shopping carts to cars, help with unloading the goods for a small tip. Meanwhile, the successful carry innumerable plastic bags filled with goods to their cars and homes: ready meals preferred. Children, who only yesterday were needed in the egumbo as herders, who were important as water carriers, and who with dance-like grace used a stick to mash millet into flour, now cling to their parents like whiny limpets who beg for sweets or money. Children who were essential to the economy of the egumbo have become beggars. And the man who used to take care of his cows is now a parking attendant who stands vigil at the edge of a parking lot and for a few cents keeps a watchful eye on the cars of Shoprite customers. If one could look at the living conditions of people and say that they have improved, it would be easier to dismiss this look at agrarian subsistence. Alas, this is not case. For many people here in the north the situation has not improved. This becomes evident when one listens to what another principal has to tell.

Observations and experiences of a principal

Timo S. is the principal of a school in the northern Namibian bush close to the Angolan border. Children go to his school from a pre-school age up until 10th grade. The school year 2012 at Timo's school starts out with 365 pupils. By mid 2013 there are still 346 – 19 children are dropouts. They gave up. Some got pregnant, some stopped showing up. In these cases, Timo contacts the children's parents and asks them to come to school, unsuccessfully for the most part. Visiting the parents is virtually impossible: The houses of the parents are difficult to reach for the principal. There is often no road leading to the huts, they are inaccessible by car. Seven of the female dropouts between age 16 and 17 got pregnant. Often it is young men from Angola, who herd cattle close to the school, who turn out to be the fathers. It is a very poor region and herders earn a little money if they herd other people's cattle. And this, according to Timo, is how they lure in the girls. Some do not have enough to eat, are hungry – and the boys take advantage of that. Girls like this, the principal explains, already have enough problems: They suffer from not having enough to eat. Now there's an additional problem in the form of pregnancy. It is a catastrophe. There is no food for the baby. And the young men return to their homes, remain vanished, and do not send money.

Whenever road builders with their machinery come to northern Namibia to flatten the gravel road then, says the principal, he can expect some girls to be pregnant afterwards. For a couple of dollar. Against hunger. Or to escape rural monotony.

The girls do not go to any medical screenings and give birth at home. Because if they go to the hospital in Eenhana to give birth, they are often turned away since they did not go there for screenings. Plus, they would have to pay for food and lodging in Eenhana themselves while waiting for the childbirth. They do, however, not have the money for that. They would have to pay around 10 Namibia dollar per day, which they cannot afford. Thus, they are dependent on the traditional midwives. Of those there are many, but they do not even use gloves, which is why there is a risk of HIV infection, says Timo. And after the birth, the girls cannot even register their babies since this is only possible if both parents sign the birth certificate.

Some girls are also impregnated by Angolan border police officers. The girls are often happy when they get pregnant this way, because they think they now have a fixed relationship and support. But the police officers are often stationed elsewhere after a time or they take other girls. And then the baby cannot be registered.

In our school, says Timo, we also accept children without birth certificates, so that they at least receive some education and a portion of maize porridge a day. But this is only possible up until the end of 9th grade. To pass the exams in the 10th grade, pupils need either a personal ID or a birth certificate.

There are also some older women and men without identification documents. They had fled to Angola during the liberation war. Then they returned at the age of 35 or 40 – without documents. In those cases, it is also difficult for their children to receive a Namibian ID. While the Namibian government does give IDs to people were born in Angola during a specific time period, people still have to be able to go to the government office for that, which often is made impossible by the associated transportation costs. And they have to speak English – otherwise (depending on the civil servant) they are turned away.

Princial Timo shows us a list with 65 names of pupils who do not have birth certificates. They will leave school without graduating.

At school, there is one meal, maize porridge, which is cooked by voluntary female helpers from the village. Sometimes, they do not show up – e.g. when there is a celebration – and then, there is nothing to eat at school. The cooks are not paid by the school. Sometimes the school gives them a little bit of maize flour. At times, the government's maize flour deliveries do not reach the school. The government provides school feeding for public primary schools, but there are constant logistics issues with the supplies, says the principal. This is especially dramatic during droughts.

Timo complains that the state aid which caretakers receive from the government to support orphans or half-orphans often is not used for the children's benefit: »Imagine there's a child here in the village and the legal caretaker who receives the money lives in Windhoek. In that case nobody makes sure that the money is invested in the child's best interest, or even that it reaches the child at all.« The guardians who receive the money have to get the school's confirmation that their child goes to school. This is because the pay-out of the money is tied to school attendance. Timo does not confirm school attendance of a child if the money is not spent on it. Three times a year this form has to be filled out. The principal regularly makes enquiries at households to see whether the money is actually sent to the village by a living parent or legal caretaker.

Special difficulties also emerge for children when a man or woman enters into a new relationship with a partner. What becomes of the children in that scenario? If a woman moves in with a new man, that man will not necessarily accept the woman's children. This is one of the situations from which child headed households are created: The mother leaves and leaves the children back at her house.

Here in the village, the principal reports, many children live with their grandmothers or other relatives, sometimes also with non-relatives. Some children live alone if they are orphans or were abandoned. Sometimes they move here without any adults to live close to the school.[120]

Children write about themselves

It was grandmothers who, during the peak of the HIV/AIDS crisis, took in most of the children who had become orphans or half-orphans. And to this day, it is mainly grandmothers who take care of children in difficult situations. Be it children who do not have parents any longer; be it that the parents live far away, or that they have entered new relationships.

Hilda is a girl like that, living with her grandmother. At the time of telling her story, Hilda is 17 years old. We asked learners of a rural and an urban school two questions respectively: First: »Who takes care of you?« Second: »Growing up in times of AIDS – what is your experience?« The learners noted down their experiences for us. Hilda's experiences with her grandmother are anything but idyllic. On the question »Who takes care of you?«, she writes:

> »I'm a 17 year old girl. I live with my grandmother. I'm hereby to give proof that the only person who is responsible for taking care of me is

---

120 Interview with Timo S., October 6, 2012, Ondangwa, Namibia.

my grandmother. The main reasons for me to be with my grandmother is that she is my father's mother. Secondly, she is near to the school where I go. I cannot stay with my mother because she is very far and where she is, there is no school. Therefore, I just have to stay with my grandmother.

I'm the only child in our house that is not with her mother. My dad is from our house, but he is working in Walvis Bay. The problem is that my father never comes to visit us. He never helped my granny, not even in buying my basic needs or paying my SDF [school development fund]. I'm just here depending on my grandmother. Granny is too old and she is also having her children. They are not working, they are just depending on her also.

Some of my needs in which granny can help me are my school needs. My grandmother ususally pays my SDF each year, but that is all when it comes to my school needs. She tells me straigt forward that she has her children to take care of. My mother is very far. I cannot get there for a weekend, I can just get there during long weekends and holidays. Mum usually buys all my basic needs, enough to reach the other coming holiday when I will be with her. My dad never gives me anything, not even a single soap.

Grandmother also provides me with enough food, but even though she does that, whenever I'm coming from holiday, I just have to carry food from my mother. Grandmother always clearly states that the house is full and she cannot afford to give enough food for everybody around her. Apart from that, with my own feeling I think that granny uses to think that she normally satisfies all my needs. But as I can see and think what is happening in my life these years, she don't really care about me as my mom would if I was staying with her.

I cannot talk about my dad, because he never gives anything to me, and he is also to be blamed of everything that happens to me while he is there in Walvis Bay.«[121]

---

121   »The house is full«. In: Fink/ Gronemeyer 2013: 51 et seq.

Hilda has clear words about her father. She shares this experience with many children in Namibia: »They don't support,« is the expression which one hears time and again when it comes to fathers. Equally bitter and accusatory are Hilda's reflections about being a child in times of AIDS:

> »Aids is the disease that made us lose many of our relatives. Nowadays some of the children in our community are suffering because they have no parents. They became orphans due to this disease.
>
> When I look around in our community, especially in houses where some parents left due to AIDS, I come to realise that they left their children in a bad situation. These children have nobody who take care of them. No one will support them with clothes and food. Those type of situations lead to poor listening at school when children are in classes. One day I went to visit my aunty in Ongwediva. There I have seen a lot of orphans. Some live with their stepmother and some with their relatives. There I realised that if one of your parents passes away and you live with someone who is not your mom or dad, it's very much difficult to survive better. Orphans are treated badly, some are being beaten up and down every day and being chased away.«

There is certainly a degree of generalisation to these statements, but the essays and interviews confirm: The misappropriation of the child welfare grant is widespread. Alcoholism among adults is often the reason for this misuse of the government-funded orphan allowance.

Paulina is 15 years old. She goes to the same school as Hilda. Her answer to the question »who takes care of you?« is very ambivalent. She also lives with her grandparents. She is grateful but at the same time emphasises that she does not feel treated well:

> »As we know, taking care is popular in our country nowadays. Those responsible for taking care of me are my parents. Unfortunately, my grandparents are the ones who take care of me. The reasons is that the house of my parents is very far from the school. Though the house of

my grandparents is not that much nearer to the school, the distance is shorter.

My grandparents give me food. I think this food is enough for me. About the school needs, my parents are the ones who pay for my school fund and buy me the uniform and everything related to the needs of the school. My grandparents are not really responsible for my shelter because sometimes I inform them about my problems, but nobody can overcome them.

I really appreciate to be with my grandparents, even though they are not really taking good care of me. I observed many mistakes they did to me, but I will thank them for being with me all the time until now.

I never received clothes from my grandparents until now, but I received food. This is possible, because they only get the pension and it is not enough for them. They sometimes say bad things to me, but I ignore it, as I know that to be taken care of by a person who is not your biological parent is very difficult.

Sometimes I do not get enough time to study due to the work that I need to do in the house, which sometimes makes me sad and think about my parents. When I'm staying with my grandparents, I am not really free because when it comes to the way that I am treated, it is different from the way they are treating their children.«[122]

In nearly every essay, the following central aspects of care are addressed: food, school fees, school uniform. Who takes care of these? Who pays? Many complain about bad treatment: »I am not happy with the way I am treated in my uncle's house.« And 17 year-old Tresia says: »Staying with my aunt is just like I am a slave«:

»Sometimes, I don't eat and, in most cases, they accuse me of everything what is done in the house. They say I am the one who did it, though I was not found in the house at that time. They always take my

---

122   »To be taken care of by a person who is not your biological parent is very difficult«. Ibid.: 55 et seq.

things, especially money, which I use to help myself. When I ask them, they nearly chase me out of their house. I do everything, pounding [*mahangu*], collecting firewood, fetching water and cooking for them, but they don't help me with anything.

I'm not happy to stay with them, it is only because I don't know where to stay as long as I'm schooling.«[123]

However, there are also cases of modest but peaceful living conditions. For example, Shangelao who is 15 years old and describes her life like this:

»I live with my biological parents in a village called Eembidi. My parents take care of me and I am enjoying living with them. They are responsible for all my needs. They make sure that there is enough food so that we cannot starve. Our staple food is omahangu [millet pap], and we depend on farming to get food. It is at substantial level.

My mother runs a Cuca shop and she tries by all means to earn money to buy food. She is responsible for doing the housework. I help her with some of the housework at the weekend and after school. My father, who is a builder, is responsible for paying my school fees and to buy stationeries that I need at school. He works hard to earn money to pay for our basic needs. I am enjoing living with my parents. They are kind and always eager to help me. They don't abuse me and, whenever I did something wrong, they take disciplinary measures that are fair and appropriate and logically related to my misbehaviour. They do not use corporal punishment as a disciplinary measure, and I am happy to live with them because I know they respect and trust me.«[124]

---

123   »Staying with my aunt is just like I am a slave«. Ibid: 62 et seq.

124   »They will not have a bright future«. Ibid.: 71 et seq.

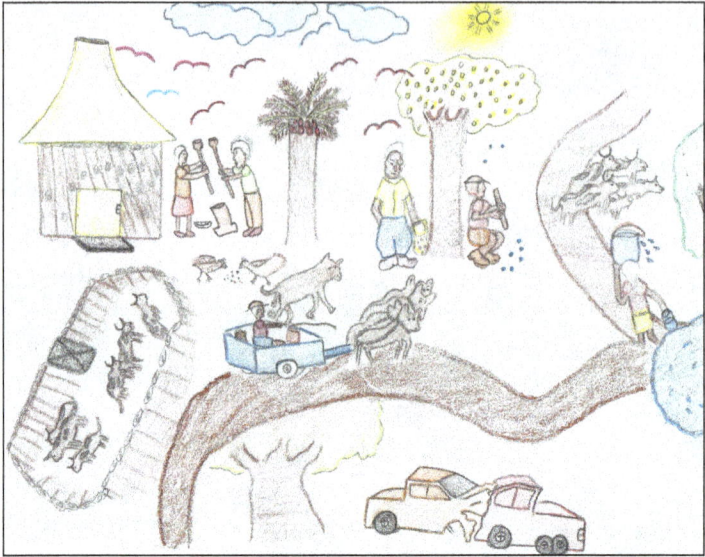

»Being a child in Ondangwa«. That is the title of these pictures which were painted in March 2020 by children at a day care centre of the Namibian aid organisation Oonte. Oonte supports 650 orphans and vulnerable children in Ondangwa, northern Namibia. The children live in Ondangwa and the surrounding villages.

Linea and her children[125]

»If any trace remains of the reputedly original thaumazein, the asto-
nished pausing in front of an unheard-of item, one can be sure that it
can be traced back to a voice from the off or the word of a layperson.
The experts just shrug and go back to their daily affairs. For no disci-
pline is this truer than for the social sciences. According to their internal
standards, one may describe them as a resolutely wonder-free zone.«[126]

Peter Sloterdijk

Linea A. stood on the small square made of compacted and smoothed
clay when her strength ran out. In the middle of the square, which is
called *oshini*, was, as usual, the hole into which she had poured the millet corns to mash them. This mashing is, or more precisely: was, the traditional preparation to cook *oshifima*, the millet porridge. Today, most
people take their millet corns to mills. For ages, *oshifima* has been the
staple food for men and women, children and old people in northern
Namibia. *Oshifima* is the foundation of life, a thick, nearly solid food
served in a plaited bowl (*elilo*) around which the family and guests, in
short: Everyone, sit and tear out pieces. These pieces are then kneaded,
mixed with (if available) spinach or chicken, and eaten. Life revolves
around *oshifima*, it is what keeps people alive, *oshifima* is the cultural
cantus firmus of the Ovambo culture. *Oshifima* is a reminder that after
the end of the Stone Age, with the beginning of arable farming, porridge started a global triumph where for many cultures it served as the
original enabler for sedentariness, familiarity, and food security.[127] The

---

125   Based on an interview with Linea A. on March 28, 2012, in the village of Omishe
        (Ohangwena Region) and years of regular visits with Linea.

126   Sloterdijk 2012: 8 (own translation of the quote).

127   According to the etymological dicitionary, the German word for porridge, »Brei«,
        refers to a viscous dish. It is assumed that the term »Brei« originally meant »the
        cooked« (»gekocht«), the »brew« (»Sud«), the German linguistic root of »Brei« re-
        ferring to »boiling up, being in heavy motion«. The word »Brei« is related to the
        terms »braten« (to roast), »brühen« (to brew), »Brot« (bread), and »brennen« (to

lump of porridge, in a sense, marked the beginning of that culture on which kingdoms and cathedrals could be built; porridge is the symbol of transition from nomadic fragility to sedentary culture.[128] And at the same time, one has to keep in mind that the latin term *cultura* originally refers to farming: The corn and the porridge are the realization, practically the nutritional concretisation, of *cultura*.[129] Culture begins with porridge.

Linea, masher in her hands, is already a symbol of progress. After all, the corn was originally ground with a round stone on a tilted, smooth stone slab. But Linea mashes: with an *omuhi*, a stake, thick as her arm, whose upper end is reinforced. The *omuhi* is raised high with

---

burn) (Pfeifer 1993: 168). In modern societies, porridge has become a dish for babies and the elderly.

»The origin of the English term ›porridge‹ on the one hand goes back to the term ›pottage‹, a variation on the French ›potage‹ – a description for soup - and on the other hand to ›pot‹, as in the cooking pot. The term ›porridge‹ may have only come into use in the 17th century, but the practice of hacking or grinding grain (e.g. oats, wheat, or corn) and boiling it in a pot with water or milk is significantly older. That is to say, the consumption of porridge-like dishes can be traced throughout the entire history of human civilisation. Researchers assume that the cooking of grain-like grasses was practised 12.000 years ago and that it went hand in hand with the transition from nomadic hunter and gatherer cultures to sedentary arable farming.« (https://verival.de/blog/geschichte-porridge, own translation of the quote).

128 The latin word *cultura* originally meant the cultivation (of fields), then expanded (from *colere*) to a religious dimension (»cult«). Since approx. 1700, there is an additional metaphorical meaning, which alludes to the training and spiritual perfection of the individual. Herder and Kant turned the word into a slogan of the Enlightenment. Ibid.: 743.

129 The fact that today nomads like the Namibian Himba have adopted the porridge into their diet is, of course, an adaption from the world of crop farmers. Remnants of the old culture of porridge can nowadays for example be found in the Northern Italian *polenta*. This cornmeal loaf had a precursor in a millet porridge, called *paniccio*, made from a millet called *panico*. In Roman times, this type of porridge was considered a staple diet (Dickie 2008: 56.). Cf. the article »Brei« in: Bächtold-Stäubli 1987: pp. 1537–1549.

both hands and then smashed down onto the corn. This is the work of women who with rhythmic movement swing the mashers until the corn has been turned into flour.

Once the flour has been ground, it is filled into a plaited bowl and carried to the cooking station. It is then cooked in a three-legged iron kettle, which sits atop three stones between which a fire smoulders. It is stirred and, finally, the porridge in poured into a plaited bowl.

On that day, *omuhi*, the masher, dropped from Linea's hands. Painstakingly, she dragged herself back to the hut. The following morning, she felt better and decided to gather fruits, only to notice she was utterly powerless. The day after, she took a basket with laundry to go wash it and herself. Doing this, she fell to the floor and was henceforth paralysed. Since 1999 she has been bedridden, since 2002 her relatives, particularly her mother, also feed her, because she cannot eat on her own anymore. She has to be carried to the toilet. She does not bear any pressure sores, no decubitus. One of her legs was swollen for a long time. Once in the fourteen years she has been confined to her bed she was taken to the hospital in Onandjokwe because of an ulcer in her breast. Afterwards, she returned to her hut. A difficult transport through the bush where there are no roads, only sandy, bumpy track grooves.

Linea, who lies on her mat, who smiles and sings, who can only move her eyes, mouth, and fingers by this point, views herself as a healthy person: »I am not sick, I just cannot walk,« she says. Linea has learned to write short SMS. Every Sunday, children from the neighbouring *omagumbo* gather at her place for Sunday school – to sing and pray together. At nights in particular, Linea feels her complete helplessness: Sometimes, rats gnaw on her toenails. A snake was also in her hut once. Snakes are what she is afraid of most.

It is not clear whether her paralysis is the result of an HIV infection. The effects of the HIV/AIDS epidemic are obvious in almost every *egumbo*. Nearly every family has lost young men or women. When it comes to this, people say »he/she died of the sickness«.

Back to Linea: Here in our country, her condition would make her a care level 3 patient, which is the highest level of care dependency and would almost inevitably result in her being taken to a nursing home. In Namibia, however, it is embedded as an, albeit difficult, still somewhat unagitated matter of course. Recently, the situation has gotten even more challenging: Since her mother Sarah had a stroke and is now care dependent, too, Linea has been in the care of one of her daughters. Linea has three children, all of whom are adolescents.

Linea's fate is tempting: She could be misused as an icon of a poor Africa in need of help, of an Africa that fails, that sinks into squalor, that is haunted by disease and poverty. If one is open to reversing the perspective, Linea reveals the direct opposite: the strength of cohesion, of solidarity in the egumbo, is made clear by the very vulnerability she displays. Linea, who thinks of herself as healthy, who does not want to go to a hospital, who is taken care of by her relatives. She who takes her modest living conditions with serenity, even, in a sense, with merriment. And Linea, who has been lying down for years, is possibly closer to freedom than the banker who after a 12-hour day at work tries to shake off the office stress in a bistro.[130] She, Linea, looks as if she were closer to death than life, but maybe looks can be deceiving?

In modern industrialised societies the question of cohesion becomes a question of survival. One must »consider the threat to social cohesion posed by the stress-free ecstasy of the subject,« writes Peter Sloterdijk. He speaks of the galley of reality constantly swinging the whip above individuals, pushing them to »self-realisation«.[131] It should

---

130   »The person who lies down is closer to freedom,« writes Peter Sloterdijk with regards to a report by Rousseau and to the stage play »Eleutheria« by Samuel Beckett. Perhaps this sentence applies to Rousseau who floats in his rowing boat and to Beckett's Viktor, who rubs his chains together (»That useless little sound, that will be my life.«), and maybe to Linea? Who knows? (Sloterdijk 2012: 52; own English translation of the first quote from the German original; for the second quote from Sloterdijk the original English-language quote from Eleutheria was used).

131   Sloterdijk 2011: 46 and 48 (own translation of the German quote).

be noted that this here is not meant to sugarcoat Linea's living conditions. Rather, it is about showing how our situation (in Europe) has long since been marked by the fact that were are »liberals«, »free people«, which by now often means nothing but that we are people who do not need each other.[132]

The cohesion in which Linea lives is the diffuse, fragile cohesion of the *egumbo* tradition, where responsibility for each other is useful – and humane. Why did Sarah and her family not discreetly dispose of Linea, which should not be too difficult given the isolation in their area? The answer, one may assume, lies in the culture of the *egumbo*.

Linea, together with her mother and their children, is a sort of placeholder in this *egumbo*. Her brother was granted this spot, as is customary, by the headman, the governor of the traditional authority. For this *plot*, he paid 600 Namibia dollar (which is around 40 USD). This land is kind of a fief, not actually a possession, but the headman is obligated to report the »purchase« to the regional authorities. By our European standards this seems fairly little money for such a large area. It was cheaper since it first had to be cleared out. Linea and her family are here to protect the area. They mark the land that her brother acquired through their presence. Should their brother marry, he will move into this *egumbo*. Before they lived here, they had erected a fence around the area, but despite this the *mahangu* field had repeatedly been ravaged by animals (goats, cows, donkeys) when they came for the harvest. This is why they now live here. But if Sarah, the mother, were to die, her burial ceremony would take place at her own *egumbo*.

---

132 Martin Walser, quoted in Sloterdijk 2011: 56.

Child labour, rural culture, and its devaluation by schools[133]

As much as there are terrible forms of child exploitation existing (especially in Africa and Asia), this judgement does not fit the traditional agrarian everyday life in Namibia. The older children get, the more involved they become in the traditional economy of the *egumbo*. They contribute because otherwise there would not be enough food. Girls and boys are involved in different, gender-specific ways. Traditionally, girls used to mash the corn: In a depression in the inner parts of the *egumbo* they poured (and sometimes still pour) millet, then smashed a long wooden staff with a thickened end onto it in order to crush it. To witnesses this labour of the girls often seemed like a dance with a masher. Afterwards, the millet porridge was cooked. Using the pot, lodged atop three stones, beneath it the fire, they constantly had to churn and whisk the porridge to make it tasty. Finding and collecting wood was also among the tasks reserved to girls and women. The collections of long branches and small wood chips were and are carried on top of their heads. Both girls and boys fetch water, which in former times was poured into earthenware jugs, now plastic containers. The water is fetched from the *lishana*, the ponds that emerge where rainwater from the rainy season gathers.

The boys were (and to some extents: continue to be) tasked with herding the cattle: cows and goats. Even today, one can encounter boys with bow and arrow in the bush, where they spend long periods of time with the animals and use their weapons to at least hunt a small extra

---

133   The international childhood research is clearly characterised by a monocultural perspective: It is a »WEIRD-Perspective«, originated from western, educated, industrialised, rich, and democratic societies. Such is the description of anthropologist David Lancy. In research as well, the »labour« of children is treated as deviance, which ought to be controlled or even abolished. In this sense, labour – as a central aspect of the lives, development, and the identity of children – is hardly acknowledged at all. In his book »Anthropological Perspectives on Children as Helpers, Workers, Artisans, and Laborers«, Lancy attempts to close this gap. See Lancy 2018.

Northern Namibia: After the rainy reason children catch fish in an oshana.

meal. They used to have knowledge of the many wild fruits and roots, which grow in the bush and can be used as food. The whole family is involved in growing millet: with ploughing and hacking, sowing the seeds, weeding, harvesting, threshing, drying, and storing. Children are also needed as helpers in the cultivation of food crops like spinach, beans, pumpkins. The same goes for the harvest of tree fruits like the *marula* fruit. During the *marula* harvest, the women and girls sit in the shade beneath trees and peel the nutty core out of the fruit pod, so that they can take the seeds of the core to produce oil. The fruits are eaten and used to brew the light fermenting white *marula* drink. The small delicious *embe* fruits have to be picked up from the ground beneath the trees. During rainy season, fish can be caught in the *lishana*; the same is true for frogs, which are gathered and dried. They are strung together with a cord and hung in the sun.

An old description illustrates the lush fertility of this *Oshana* region:

>North of the aforementioned arid areas the stoneless Amboland
stretches until the Kunene. It forms a tremendous plain interspersed
with gentle bumps. In good rain years the waters of the Kunene and
Okawanga flow deep into Amboland and into odd depressions, thus
enabling arable farming and fishing. The expanses offer lush pastures.
The well-fortified and cleanly kept farmsteads of the indigenous tend
to be situated on the elevated ridges of land. Enormous baobab trees,
shady fig trees, and imposing fan palms create a rather picturesque
and friendly landscape.« [134]

This traditional agrarian world is fading away like snow in the sun.
Coming from the new urban centres, modern life grasps for this traditional way of life and devalues it. The urban clinic makes the traditional
healer, the *nanga*, out to be a charlatan (even though many people still
go to the *nanga*). Knowledge about herbs with healing properties is disappearing, in part also due to the fact that these become increasingly
hard to find. The pill is more credible anyway. Toast and soft drinks
degrade *oshifima* (millet porridge) and *ontaku* (a nutritious children's
drink made from millet). The authority of the elders is undermined
since the signals the young ones receive from the modern world are
stronger. They do not obey anymore, complain the elders.

But more than anything it is the school: No instrument of the modern world flips the structure of smallfarming lifeworlds on its head
quite as radically as the school. Children are turned from contributors
to the homestead economy to objects of professional lecturing at separate locations. This drains their labour force from the egumbo. They
are not there any longer to collect wood, fetch water, herd the cattle,
cook *oshifima*. Some things are still possible before or after school. But

---

134   According to Vedder 1934: 4. It should be noted that Vedder's descriptions may
      historically not always have been reliable (according to Wallace 2011) (own trans-
      lation of the German quote).

it is not uncommon for students to walk home for more than an hour, and by then they should do their homework. Or they live in a hostel and only return home on weekends or during the holidays. They lose their domestic and agrarian skills. And, in essence, they lose their groundedness: They envision themselves as nurses, pilots, doctors, teachers, lawyers, police officers – but not as farmers. Regardless of the fact that most of them do not graduate. And as for those who do graduate but then cannot find work: They do not fit into the *egumbo* anymore. And the adults feel this. On the one hand, the elders associate their children going to school with hope, on the other hand school devalues agrarian life and labour. They, i.e. the farmers, are no longer regarded as the ones who can provide for their own livelihood; but they are the degraded, the disqualified, the uneducated: those who did not (or only for a few years) go to school, who only know how to plant millet and drink the traditional beer. They represent the past while the children are, well, they are the sham future, because many march towards a dead end, since the poor job market cannot accommodate the many young people looking for employment.

In a settlement of the Damara in Sesfontein, in northern Namibia, a small group of children in yellow school uniform is standing atop a hill. They watch as a group of elder, clad in animal furs, do traditional healing dances. The Damara are among the most marginalised groups in Namibia. They subsist on breeding goats and sheep, on day labour or farm jobs, and on the small old-age pensions, which the state pays to every person past the age of 60. The elderly want to pass on their traditions to the children. They maintain their customs and on special occasions dress in the furs that their ancestors wore.

The old and the new garments – school uniform and furs – reveal an insurmountable contrast. The school children stand in the background of the scenery and look down on the old, which probably has little chance of survival. They represent modernity – like the burger, they are a global product. The old is thus replaced with a universal monoculture. The elderly say: »If we do not pass on our culture, our roots to our children, then life ends.«[135]

The 2010 documentary »Schooling the World«[136] paints a devastating picture of global schooling. It questions the programmatic claim that education reduces poverty and claims the opposite: that school takes millions of young people out of their local community, culture, and economy – in which they used to have a modest but dignified livelihood – and sparks in them a desire for an urban, consumerist lifestyle, which remains unattainable for most. In doing so, school produces more and more people who stray between worlds. In the film, Indian researcher and activist Vandana Shiva refers to these people as »in-between people«: millions who become slum dwellers and losers of the system.[137]

The market, the garbage, the millet. Three zones in an African city. Three lifestyles of children

Ondangwa is a city in the north of Namibia. Or, actually, it is debatable whether Ondangwa can properly be labelled a city. Ondangwa is rather a motley collection of gas stations, malls, banks, and fast food restaurants latching onto the sides of a tarred road, the B1, which connects Namibia's north with the capital, Windhoek. Everything that used to characterise a city (polis) has been eliminated here. The road, a thick pulsating vein, serves the exclusive purpose of establishing contact between goods and people. Vast parking spaces stretch left and right to the road, surrounded by a u-shape of concrete and plastic edifices. Markets, markets, markets out of which people, reduced to their functions as customers, push their purchases in carts. The buildings are nothing but vessels for goods and they look accordingly. At the exit of

---

135 Our own observations and talks in a Damara community in Sesfontein, Namibia, 2017.

136 Schooling the world 2010: https://schoolingtheworld.org/film.

137 See also Fink 2019.

the supermarkets you always find long rows of cash registers, where plastic-sealed industrial food moves across conveyor belts: The unveiled, naked way in which goods and buyers come face to face evokes images of Dante's description of hell. And, by the way, everything in these halls looks as if it were made to be razed tomorrow. A rat scuttles hurriedly beneath a vegetable shelf. A sack of potatoes, upon closer inspection revealed to be swarming with cockroaches – these are the small holes of modernity. They remind us of the speed with which modernity fell upon these people: At most, it is ragged around the edges, and it is there that perfection is not yet seamless.

The devastations of war are sometimes still recognisable in the landscape: For example, the remnants of a wall on the grounds of a school near Epinga, not far from Ondangwa. It is littered with bullet holes. It is a remnant of a school that was destroyed in the war and left there as a memorial.

Are the new malls and the explosively blossoming opportunities for consumerism a form of scab growing over the wounds inflicted by Apartheid and the war? Is this nearly seamless transition from the bloody war into consumerist modernity part of a healing process? Are these concrete shopping gulches perhaps about life and survival, about enjoyment and rebuilding, about shopping, consuming, music, about mobility, about the mobile phone? About the »after«? In other words, about the healing over of wounds and about letting scab build? Is what we see here deliberate forgetfulness?

But the bustle of buyers in the malls cannot distract from the fact that surrounding this first circle of new wealth with its chaotic, dazzling lifestyle are two outer circles: the circle of those failed existences who, stuck between the new centres of growth and the old agrarian lifeworld, struggle for basic survival. And the additional circle inhabited by those who try to maintain the small farmer lifestyle, which is getting increasingly eroded.

Just a few hundred metres away from the often clogged, consumer-serving B1 vein, one can enter into an utterly different realm. An area dominated by sand, shacks, and poverty. There, one can find a grey-

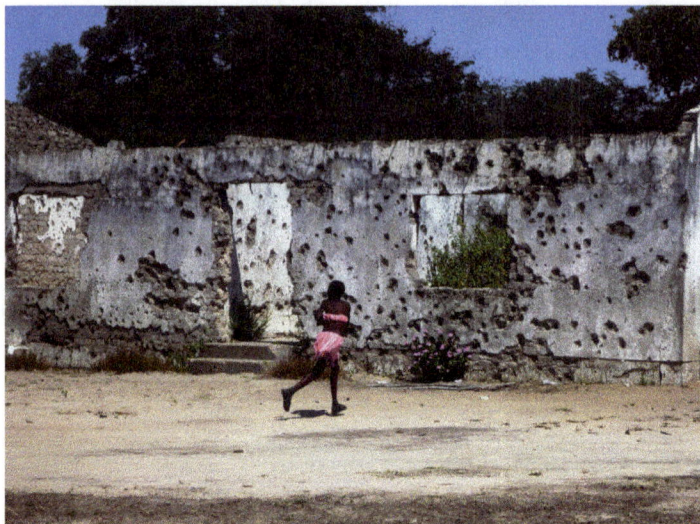

Memorial: The bullet-riddled walls of an old school building belonging to the Shimbode School in the village of Epinga in the northern Namibian Ohangwena region. This area, close to the Angolan border, saw some of the heaviest fighting during the years of the liberation war.

haired grandmother, her emaciated frame clad in the red-pink dress that female farmers traditionally wear. She stands in front of her hut in the outskirts of Ondangwa together with seven children. They are her grandchildren; her daughters work in Walvis Bay. She lives on her old-age pension. Every now and then, her daughters send some money. She has a nice millet field right next to her hut. Cultivating millet – that is a lifesaving habit she brought with her from the countryside to the urbanised poverty belt around Ondangwa. Meanwhile, the city has fenced in the field with tall wire. The city took it from her, bought it off for an (enforced) knockdown price. Because the city is growing, and this millet field now occupies precious building land. Eventually, she will also have to vacate her hut, only to erect it anew some distance away. In the no man's land which one day is probably also going to be-

come building land. Step by step, the suburbs of Ondangwa thus de-
vour the remnants of agrarian subsistence. The elderly with children,
the failed ones, they have to make way, to be thankful if they even have
enough money to shop at the remaining informal markets. There, they
buy blankets and mattresses, if they can, at Chinese stores. The Namibian buyers know all too well that the expiration time of these products is short, but they cannot afford anything more long-lived.

Within the second circle around Ondangwa's economic urban
centre lies Victoria's property. Cut off from agrarian subsistence and
at the same time without income from old-age pension or a job, she
dwells within nothingness together with her family. For as far as the
eye can see plastic bags litter the ground, a few struggling grass blades
peeking through. From time to time, there's a lean cow chewing on
a plastic bag. Victoria sits on an upended, damaged beer crate. She
wears a dress full of holes, the right shoulder of the garment hangs
torn. Her mother lies on a shredded foam rubber mattress, wearing
rags. She is drunk, the canister next to her is filled with *tombo*, the traditional homebrewed millet beer. The place is littered with all kinds
of rubbish. Victoria collects scrap to try and earn some money. Rusty
casks, cans, canisters, tyres – everything in wild disarray. A few won-
ky chairs, lacking everything that makes a chair a chair, lean against
the wall of the shack in which the family sleeps. Skeleton chairs.

We are visitors, balancing on those skeleton chairs. We sit across
from Victoria; her children are next to her in the sand. Skin and clothes
are covered in dust. A boy (maybe three years old) has grabbed his foot
and tries to remove a splinter from it using a rusty nail. Next to him
sits a small girl who tears pages from a tattered song book. Some distance away, a girl has wrapped an originally white strip of cloth around
her like a ballerina. Grace amidst garbage.

And yet: Despite or because of this bleak scenery, the spark of vitality, of zest for life emitted by these children catches the eye. Everything
points to them being cut-offs. Cut off from good food, good clothing,
good education – and it seems as if amidst these terrific living conditions this surprising brilliant vitality is born.

In the inner first circle of Ondangwa children become used to throw-away clothes, fast food, and plastic toys; within the poverty belt, the second circle, children have adapted to uncertain food supply, life amidst sand, rags, and plastic rubbish. Meanwhile, the children in the third circle find themselves in the traditional rural farmer world. In the *egumbo* (see the description in chapter 2), the farmstead surrounded by palisades, which encompasses huts with different social meanings: the girls' hut, the one for boys, for the wife, the husband, for cooking, for chicken, for brewing beer, for supplies etc. What once used to be a mostly modest, subsistent agrarian way of life survives – as mentioned previously – only in fragments. The men are part of the wage labour force, work sometimes thousands of kilometres away, rarely return home. Sometimes only once per year. This third circle in the area of the egumbo is often only accessible through the sand tracks, but news of the modern world in Ondangwa has reached every egumbo anyway. Even if it is just due to many of the HIV positive people fetching their medication there. Plus, the mobile phone serves as a connection to this world. The children's longing is directed at the things available there, but for which there is no money.

Children who grew up in this traditional agrarian world were no deficient creatures in need of education but contributors as far as their capabilities allowed. It was fortunate that many children lived in the *egumbo*. Because this laid the foundation that guaranteed current and future well-being. As long as they were carried on the backs of their mothers as babies, they were free of duties. They were carried around during the cooking, during fieldwork, they were there when the women were talking. They were integrated into the daily rhythms of life, only put down to sleep or feed. And while being carried in such a way, they had a chance to look over the mother's shoulder (while in our culture the pram forces the child's gaze onto the mother or father who pushes it).

As soon as they could walk, they were put under the care of older siblings. And brought close to their first duties. An unforgettable case: the three-year-old Himba boy who the foreman of the farmstead »gifted« to a blind old Ovambo man as a companion. The Himba live in the northwest of Namibia in a nearly Stone Age nomadic lifestyle – which is dissolving rapidly. This boy led the old man and there was evidently an almost tender relation between these two people.

Northern Namibia, at a Himba farmstead: a retired worker (he is Ovambo and blind) and the small companion who has been assigned to him.

III. Children in Urban Katutura

Kabashu: The situation of children in Silvertown

Northern Namibia has been suffering from persistent rural exodus to the cities, especially, of course, to Windhoek, or more specifically: to Katutura. Many children live with their grandparents on the country-side while the adults try to earn money in Windhoek or at other places. There is a continuous back and forth between the Namibian north and urban Katutura.[138] Those who are old or care-dependent go back to the north if they can. Up until now, many people from other regions are still buried in the north – a costly affair, but one which people still pay for if possible.

Within the context of this migration, which generally works both ways, a remarkable cultural amalgamation is created, incorporating traditional orientations and radical modernity – a feature which to many does not seem difficult at all. This is exemplified by a young man who is not Ovambo but Herero. He displays that skill which character-ises many Namibians, namely the ability to handle elements of tradi-tional culture and the modern world with equal ease. Nelson Mbend-jipa was born in 1984 in Okakarara, the native territory of the Herero. If he can find a job, Nelson earns his money as a web designer. At the same time, he worries about how he is supposed to find a wife who can look after the domestic holy fire. Obviously, to this day this holy fire continues to be of great importance to the Herero. In any event, the cultural mix in Nelson's case is remarkable:

---

138 On city-countryside-relations see e.g. Tvedten 2011.

>When I get married, Windhoek will be just a place for employement. But my place will be in the village. The village is in Okakarara district. So for Windhoek we only come for school and employment.«[139]

At the same time, he recounts how his father took him from his biological mother at the age of four months. Two children of the mother had died. To their culture, Nelson explains, this signifies that »there is a bad spirit«. This is viewed as the reason for the children's death. And thus, he was, as he tells it, adopted by his stepmother at the age of four months. Nelson still carries a traditional name: *Mbendjipa*, which translates to something along the lines of »gift of the ancestors«. Nelson explains that growing up with a stepmother like he did is nothing uncommon in Herero culture: »Every woman is just your mother.« He differentiates between his biological mother who gave birth to him, and his stepmother who raised him. When his stepmother died, he went to a female cousin. He describes himself at that time as a spoiled small boy who did not even have to go to the cattle kraal to milk animals. Nelson was used to wait during meals until someone brought him food and later took his dishes away for washing. His cousin immediately changed this:

>At the first weekend when I went there she told me that, ›okay, it's fine, I will wash your clothes for now, but after this weekend you have to do it for yourself. Because what if I pass away, who will take care of hat?‹«[140]

Evidently, this familial flexibility can also cause breaches in terms of sudden changes in education styles, changes of locations, changing habits. Nelson went to school but did not use the money he received from his father for school, instead spending it for himself. He lost his schoolbooks. The school refused to grant him a certificate as long as he

---

139 Interview with Nelson M., March 24, 2013, Katutura.
140 Ibid.

had not paid his debts. Somehow, he finally managed to receive training as a web designer. From time to time, he has a job in Windhoek, where he lives now. He astutely describes the cultural differences:

> »I feel there is a loss of our cultural roots. Most children grow up in the city now, where we have multiple cultures. [...] We copy from other cultures. And we have modern technologies, television and whatever. So we adapt the culture from other continents like Europe. Now we are dressing the way we want to dress. But when you go home, it's different. Your parents will feel bad really; you hurt them in one or the other way.«[141]

One cannot marry a girl from another culture, because she is not welcome at the holy fire. There are traditional beverages and four different traditional vessels, calabashes, whose distinct purposes must be respected. There are calabashes for visitors, while others are purely reserved for the family. Here in Windhoek, Nelson says, I can have girlfriends from other tribes. However, my father wishes that I replace him as keeper of the holy fire – and that means I cannot marry anyone who is not Herero.

> »According to our culture I will replace my father, so I have to know that at the end the wife that I must have has to be someone who can also take care of the holy fire.«[142]

It is perhaps debatable whether the ties to traditional culture are as strong as Nelson claims. Nelson, the modern urbanite, or *Mbendjipa*, the Herero boy: Either way, the final sentence of the interview, where he speaks about his Okakarara home village, are unambiguous: »I don't

141 Ibid.
142 Ibid.

think there is any other beautiful place than the place where you grew up. So, that one is definetley the most beautiful place in the world.«[143]

Adults and children alike are confronted with drastic cultural rifts when they transition between urban and rural areas, between the tranquil bushland countryside of the north and lively, anarchical Katutura. This is simultaneously also the transition between (remaining) traditional culture and modern culture, which is infested with global tendencies and trends.

One example of the still strong ties to their rural origins in spite of the allure of the urban comes in the form of a reaction by a group of parents (or caretakers) at a Katutura kindergarten. Upon being asked where they feel at home, here, in the township, or there, in the north, the unanimous answer is: »It's there!«

»Silvertown« is what the locals call the settlements in Katutura where countless rows upon rows of silver-coloured corrugated-iron shacks stretch across the hills. Is it a slum? A home? A place of anarchy? A moloch or a source of creativity? Definitely a place where the overwhelming genuine power of people is revealed, who out of nothing, without government aid, nearly always without money or secure incomes, carve out modest lives for themselves. Here, everything is lacking, yet everything is there. Newcomers from rural regions erect shelters on patches of desert. From cardboard, fish cans, and other types of scrap – those who are well-situated from whole panes of corrugated-iron. And these diverse ensembles of shacks crawl up the hills and from there continue to sprawl on and on. Katutura grows and grows. Several hundred thousand people have set themselves up here, manage their daily affairs, persist in the face of hardship and adversity. There are no building authorities, no architects, no structural engineers who give counsel or regulate. The newcomers have no access to running water, electricity, or the sewer system. It is the same for most others there, including those who have been there longer. At some point, people scrounge up enough money to afford a black plastic

---

143 Ibid.

Silvertown – this is what the residents call the shantytowns of Katutura.

sheet behind which they can wash themselves and shower, which is to say: pour a bucket of water of their heads. And yes, the water has to be fetched first. If one is lucky, the pump where water is poured from is not too far away. That being said, water can only be fetched with a recharchable chip card, since it has to be bought. In many cases, there is barely enough money to buy water for drinking and cooking – water for laundry is already difficult to afford in addition to that.

The huts do not have proper floors, it is just bare ground. (Those who have been there longer may be able to afford a concrete floor, which then is considered a mark of prosperity.) On the ground, there is often just a single mattress on a bedstead, the shared sleeping place of all who live in the hut. There may be a few other possessions strewn across the floor. Perhaps a sack of maize flour. A clothesline hung with clothes. Outside, in front of the door, a »kitchen«: a few dishes (battered enamel), the plastic bowl, the sooty iron kettle on the fireplace made of three stones. Ash, wood chips. At least the hut provides some shelter. During the summer it is too hot inside, during winter it is too cold – lucky are those who own a wool blanket. If it rains, the water often pours into the hut from the sides – sometimes also from the top. During rainy season, those who can afford it get a robust tarpaulin, throw it over their hut, and weigh it down with stones so that the wind does not carry it away.

There are considerable social differences between people in Katutura, which also date back to the history of the place.[144] The name Katutura stems from the Herero language. It roughly translates to: »The place where we do not want to live«. This name points to the creation of Katutura. During Apartheid, the government planned to make Windhoek a city purely for White people. Non-White people who worked or lived in Windhoek would be banned to the outskirts of town. At that time, the so-called »old location« (in today's Hochland Park) had been the residential area of many Black people. In the 1960s, a new residential area (Katutura) was created 10 kilometres outside of Windhoek

---

144   Cf. Wikipedia under »Katutura«; Pendleton 1974.

and, at the time, separated from Windhoek by a stretch of wasteland. Today, both cities are merging. Plans for Katutura included schools, malls, and hospitals and it was built for different ethnic groups (Ovambo, Herero, Damara etc.). The standardised houses were a size of 45 square metres each. Khomasdal was for the »coloureds«. The forced relocation of Black people from the city began in 1959. On December 10, an uprising erupted in the old location. 11 protesters were killed, 44 injured. It was this protest, which eventually birthed the SWAPO. Sam Nujoma, who would go on to become the first president of independent Namibia, was involved in the protest.[145]

A staggering number of people have been moving to Katutura in the course of recent years' rural exodus. The administration tries to keep up with correspond infrastructure building, but electrification, water supplies, schools, garbage disposal, and road construction have so far only been realised in parts of Katutura.

There are also people in Katutura who are economically and socially well situated. We, however, look at vulnerable people and children in difficult circumstances. An unforgettable experience in this vein was our visit with Ottilie who is one of the poor, marginalised, hopeless.

Her name is actually Ottilie

In Goethe's »Elective Affinities« Ottilie is a destitute relative of the well-situated noble Charlotte. Her unfortunate love with Charlotte's husband, Eduard, sees her dead: She starves herself to death. Goethe's understanding of the passionately unhappy unions, which he writes about is chemical in nature: As chemical elements are moved by repulsion and attraction (the term affinity is also used to describe this phenomenon in chemistry), so are the four protagonists in Goethe's novel.

In Namibia, in Windhoek, in Katutura, in the rundown Havana district, we meet a starving Ottilie. The name Ottilie is probably a

---

145   Cf. Melber 2016.

remnant of German colonial times. It was probably a reference to Saint Odile, the saint patroness of good eyesight. The Namibian Ottilie is as delicate and beautiful as the one we are introduced to in Goethe's Elective Affinities. She sits in her small shack, which measures three by three metres. Her youngest child, a baby, is tied to her back with a piece of cloth. Ottilie has three children, and she is 34 years old. The bed on which she sits is shared by the four of them. She got the washed-out curtains, which cover the corrugated-iron walls from a garbage dump. After her husband died, his family evicted her from her home. One of her relatives left her this poor refuge. If not for this, she would have been homeless. She does not have any official documents and therefore does not receive any state welfare for her children who are half-orphans. She was born in Namibia. Her family moved to Angola and later returned, without identification documents. Technically, she is now stateless and without income, all of which means that each day it is uncertain how she will get by without letting herself and her children starve. Her kitchen consists of three stones in front of her hut between which a fire smoulders. The iron pot next to it is empty. A few wooden stakes and a piece of cardboard mark the place where she cleans herself. Which is something she cannot afford to do often. She talks about her life and soon raises her hands in front of her eyes, because she is ashamed of her tears. And, by the way: She also suffers from tuberculosis. She takes pills against that.

Once again: the voices of children

Milka sits in front of her shack in Katutura. One room, a mattress on the floor, dishes, kitchen utensils in a corner in front of the hut. Milka comes from the Namibian south. Ghinaxas is the name of her home village. She is one of the Nama people. She has three children, works as a cleaning lady at a school. She came to Windhoek looking for work. She complains that it is very difficult to earn enough money to support

her children. But even more than that, she insists that in times of the
AIDS epidemic it would be necessary to educate parents:

> »Here in Namibia many parents are too young to support the children.
> We have to start with the parents. We have to educate them: They have
> to learn how to raise a child, because not everyone knows how to take
> care of a child. And then, after a month, they are dumping the children
> or leave them with the grandparents. And that ist the biggest problem
> here in Namibia. You have to be educated before you get a child.«[146]

This is how Milka puts it, and she alludes to the large number of girls
who become pregnant at a young age. She would know of the old social relationships in the north and south of the country, which used to
have knowledge about how to raise children, where habits were passed
on and people lived in extended families. She would also know that
these embeddings have disappeared. And so, today young mothers are
left to their own devices. The disappearance of norms and guidelines
seems to be all-encompassing: »Young girls get pregnant. And when
they do get pregnant, the fathers are running away.«[147] And who knows,
says Milka, if my husband does not go out and father a child somewhere else? He would not tell me. And the child would grow up on the
street. In the best case, the grandparents would take care of it. And
thus, Milka concludes: »The government must take care of the people,
it has to look after the children.«

One has to bear in mind that this notion that childcare is a task of
the government can only come into existence from within the ruins of
old orders and a position of utter helplessness. What about the young
girl who was raped and does not even have the money to afford a birth
certificate? Milka grew up in a family with twelve children. But back
then, this was manageable, she says. There was food and school did not

---

146   Interview with Milka B., Katutura, March 23, 2013.
147   Ibid.

cost much. Seven out of twelve children went to school. Two did not graduate, three were dropouts. (These said: »We do not need school.«)

So, Milka describes what is happening: The traditional ways of dealing with children have disappeared, which is reflected in the fractioning of familial constellations in Katutura. But at the same time, Katutura reveals the incredible vitality of adults and children as well as their determination to faces the challenges of a difficult daily life.

We also asked students at the Havana Primary School to describe their situation in life: »Who takes care of you?« »What are your experiences with the topic HIV/AIDS?« The essays were written in 2012. Since then, the topic has lost some of its prominence in the public sphere. But that, of course, does not mean that it has resolved itself. However, antiretroviral drugs have managed to reduce the number of casualties and turned a deadly disease into a chronic one. In any event, today the AIDS orphan issue is not as much out in the open as a drastic issue. Rather, it has essentially expanded to become the topic of vulnerable children.

Whether in the north or in Katutura: The children describe their circumstances with great clarity. Take, for example, Victoria, a girl in 7th grade, who speaks about losses in her family, specifically the death of her father:

> »In 2000, we went to Karas when my father was sick. My father died in 2002, when I was only two years old. I always used to ask my mother when dad is coming back, but she only told me that he went to the north.
> In 2004, we went to the north. There my grandmother told me that my father was dead because I always used to ask my grandmother. I didn't know what death was. I would always ask my granny ›What is death?‹, but my grandmother would get tired and tell me to stop asking her questions.«

And she continues:

»In 2005, we went to Windhoek. My mother was struggling with work. She got work as a security guard. She called my aunt to take care of me. My aunt always used to tell me that she was sick and she was telling me about HIV. I started asking her questions while mom was there, but my aunt didn't answer me. My mother heard that my aunt was always telling me about her illness, and my mother got angry. She warned my aunt to stop telling me about her illness.

In 2006, my aunt died of HIV, and there was no one to take care of me. My mother took me to Katima Mulilo to her cousin. I started grade 1 there. My mother's cousin was treating me badly.

In 2007, I went back to Windhoek to continue with grade 2. In February 2007, my mother lost her job and was again struggling with work. In April, she got work at Ramatex. My mother got a baby boy in August. I was very angry because I was the last born and I was treated very good. But when my mother got a baby boy, I was not treated very good.

In 2008, my mother's cousin's firstborn died. When I went to the funeral, I saw people crying, and I was askin myself: Why are they crying if she went to rest? I though so because my aunt used to tell me that my father went to rest. So I thought the same about my cousing that she also went to rest. Then, my mother told me about death until I understood what death is. I realised my father also died. I was sitting in my room, holding ma father's photos, crying. My mother told me to stop crying for my father because he would bever come back again. But I didn't want to understand because I missed him so much.

In 2009, my friend's mother also died. When I told my mother she told me again about death until I understood. My mother and my stepfather are always arguing at night. In March, my mother broke up with my stepfather.«[148]

The particular pain of the child in this story is equally as palpable as the fact that AIDS-related experiences of death and confusions of familial situation have become normal for many children. Another

---

148   »My mother tried hard to take care of us«. In: Fink/Gronemeyer 2013: 3.

thing that seems to be normal for many is the transition between times in the rural north and stays at urban Katutura. The same can be said for changes in caretakers: father, mother, aunt, grandmother, brother, uncle – these are all possibilities. The fragility of work relations, the simple, often squalid living conditions in »Silvertown«, and the worry about how to satisfy basic needs are all present: Who takes care of food? Who buys the school uniform? Who pays the school fees? (Those were abolished later, after the creation of the children's essays. But in 2019, when the country faced a recession and the near bankruptcy of the state, discussions about reinstating them were held anew.)

Shipena, 12 years old, writes: »We don't have electricity, we only use candles and cooking gas. My mother is working at Katutura central hospital and my father is a policeman. [...] My mother is suffering so much about food.«[149] And Shipena tells us about that which many children obviously fall victim to: violence, rape – men, teachers, uncles, sugar daddies – the offenders are everywhere. We do not know how frequent this was in the traditional way of life. Nevertheless, the stories, press reportage, trials – and the number of pregnant girls all indicate that the destruction of traditional ways of life and norms has released a new type of violence: one that targets children – girls in particular – and defencelessly exposes them to other people's greed and grasps. In a world where every mall conveys the notion that everything is purchasable, it seems obvious to assume that money could also buy the bodies of children. And those who have no money feel prompted to use violence to fulfil that which the consumerist world preaches: that everything is attainable.

One thing the subsistent agrarian lifeworld, whose resonance can still be traced northern Namibia, did, was confront people with limits – with regards to living, mobility, their food, along with regulations pertaining to social affairs and community. This was no idyll, it was not

---

149 »Mommy, money«. In: Fink/Gronemeyer 2013: 5.

always just, but it did prevent this self-service mentality, which today turns countless children in Katutura into victims of sexual violence. Reading between the lines in Shipena's essay, one can find remarks about the reality and shape of this violence:

>»There was a girl called Martha. This girl was 12 years old. She was coming from school, and one man told her, ›Let's go an I will buy for you a sweet‹, and the girl said, ›Ok‹, and they went to the man's house. He opened the door and they went in. The man was having a sweet and he gave it to the girl and was taking the girl's clothes off. Then they did their work. When the girl felt that she has pain, she was running away, whispering ›Help, help‹. The people who found her helped her. They called the police and the police asked him, ›Why did you rape the girl?‹ But he did not answer.«[150]

The gift of astute observation and the empathic skills that children may possess are put on display in Tangeni's (6th grade) essay: »I don't have any money, I can only help with my own hands.«[151] What a sentence this is, how much recognition does it encompass! And then there is this sketch of a wretched, humiliating life, which she has come across:

>»Angula is the one having the virus. [...] The way he is living is not good. He is thin and noone gives him food. He lives in the bush because his family chased him away because he has HIV. [...] I am not happy because he is still a child. He lost many things – his friends, his parents. Er droped the school because the learners called im ›disease‹, and his

150 Ibid.

151 From an unpublished essay by a student at Havana Primary School, Windhoek. In the book »Who takes care?« (Fink/Gronemeyer 2013), only a selection of the total 170 essays in English were published.

parents did not want to pay for his school, and they were never buying something for him.«[152]

Segeria – also in 6th grade – speaks about her mother's struggle. And she herself is part of this struggle to survive: It is she who cooks for the family, a family which is evidently constantly scraping by the subsistence level:

> »My mother is suffering all the time. She is struggling to find a job but she can't find a job. She is now selling pork meat at Monte Christo road where people are selling. She earns money by selling. If she would not do that she would not survive because there is no way she can get money for us for school and for food.«[153]

These children know plenty about how serious life can be. They know that having something to eat each day is not self-evident and that children may have to contribute so that everyone's basic needs can be met. This is also Synthia's reality. She is also 12 years old and questions of survival are at the centre of her experiences. She has precise ideas of how could be implemented to reality:

> »My mother gives me food every day. And if there is no food at home she taught us how to make money by doing easy work like sweeping somebody's house and get money, taking care of somebody's car and wash it, and also by selling photo frames that we make from boxes and fire matches. [...] I feel courage as a young person to prevent deaths of our beloved. And the only key to this is to study and to become a doctor.«[154]

---

152 Excerpt from another unpublished essay by a student at Havana Primary School, Windhoek.
153 Ibid.
154 Ibid.

Synthia dreams of a bright future – as a doctor. Anna, 12 years old, describes the scenery at the time in Havana. Against this background, Synthia's dreams unfold:

>»We are staying at a dirty and dark place. There is no electricity and there are many strangers or thieves. We are staying at a deep, deep place with no electricity.«[155]

For some children, the daily life in Katutura is indeed grim – as Tresia lets us know when she writes the following about her domestic life:

>»Sometimes they want me to do everything, even to cook. When I finish to cook they chase me out and close the door, so that they can eat all themselves.«[156]

Almost laconically, Thomas (12 years old) speaks about life with his father and when visiting him he has to return with a sack full of millet:

>»I am staying with my father in Windhoek. My mother stays at the north. Now my father is the only one who takes care of me. He pays for my school. He buys me food to eat and clothes. When I come back from the north, I come with *omahangu* [millet] to cook porridge. When I am sick my father takes me to the hospital. If I do something bad my father will beat me.«[157]

His sister is one of the affected:

>»My sister is the one who was infected with the virus. She was 15 years old. She was in grade 8. When she walks in the street people start laughing. She was feeling angry. She was lazy. Her parents chased her out

---

155 Ibid.
156 Ibid.
157 Ibid.

of the house. She was a thin person who was feeling crazy. She was a street kid. She started going to the hospital. She came back home. Now she is a big girl. She left school.«

A whole life, a dramatic life, is conveyed in her brother's lines. But there is also something like normalcy, a life with an adult who takes care of things; a normalcy in which the dictates of traditional customs are evident. In this vein, 13-year-old Johannes writes:

»My mother cares for me very well. She is the one who buys food for me, clothes, and she pays for me the school. I love her. She also buys for me the school unifrom. She likes me very much. She likes a clean place and a clean person. Everyday when she comes from work, she tells us to clean the yard and wipe in the house and wash the dishes [...]. She workes at Polytec of Namibia [which is today the Namibia University of Science and Technology]. She always tells us to learn and pass our grade and start working and help her when she grows old.
She does not beat us. She only beats us when we do somthing wrong. And because she likes us and when you pass school she buys us something that we want. She likes us eating healthy food. She does not like untidy things. When we are sick she brings us to the hospital. And she doesn't like insulting words. If you insult someone she will be angry with you and tell you not to insult someone.«[158]

Bernadus, 12 years old: »I respect my parents because they do good things to me. They teach me many things that I don't know. I love my parents.«[159] Conceivable life, inconceivable life – everything is encompassed in the voices of these children: tales of daily horrors and of experiences of reliable affection, both often right next to each other as in Helena's case:

---

158 Ibid.
159 Ibid.

»My father takes care of me. He always does everything I need. He is always the one who buys for me pens and books. My uncle is working, but he just stays in the bar and drinks. When he comes home, he wants to beat me. I don't know why he is doing this. I told my mother, but she sais that I must let him and do what he wants.«[160]

Excursus: The very last desert. Children graves

Hilma was left to die by her mother. The baby was HIV-positive. She thought the child would not make it anyway. A neighbour found Hilma. After many weeks in the hospital and good nursing by the neighbour who took in the baby, Hilma is now better. The entirety of today's Namibia is contained in this story: the desperation of the mother. And the other, the life-positive, decision of the neighbour. The woman who saves the child, takes it in, and keeps it alive. A story of death and resurrection. Such is daily life together: the abandonment of many people and then this unexpected, surprising humanity and warmth, that saves that child in the last moment from the verge of death. The empathic and involved social worker from the Ministry of Gender Equality and Child Welfare says that Katutura is in dire need of a shelter for abandoned and orphaned babies. There are too many desperate and sick mothers. They would need a place where these mothers could take their children. At the State Hospital, overworked nurses and doctors are out of ideas on what to do with abandoned, malnourished, sick small children. Without medicine, without time, without support. After all, they cannot stay at the hospital.

Those who visit the large cemetery in Katutura will see the large area for children graves. Desert sand, piled up to a small hill. A plastic flower or a coca cola can, shoved into the sand as a final memory. It is not uncommon for these children to find their rest here after a

---

160 »When he comes home, he wants to beat me«. In: Fink/Gronemeyer 2013: 9 et seq.

short life. Often anonymously. Unaccompanied. Sometimes there is a
mother, a familiar, a relative at a grave. Elias Canetti, who visited the
Jewish cemetery in Marrakesh, described a similar place:

> »I found myself at an incredibly bleak place where not a single stalk
> grew. The tombstones were so low that one could nearly overlook
> them. [...] The cemetery looked like a giant pile of rubble; maybe that
> is what it had once been, and it had only later been made into what it
> now was.«

Cemeteries in other parts of the world, says Canetti, were designed so
as to bestow happiness upon the living. There, you would find plants
and birds and visitors could feel encouraged and invigorated among
so many dead.

> »His own condition seems enviable to him. On the tombstones, he re-
> ads the names of people; each one he has survived. On this desolate
> Jewish cemetery, however, there is nothing. It is truth itself, a moon-
> scape of death. [...] It is the desert of the dead, where nothing grows any
> longer, the last, the final desert.«[161]

---

161   Canetti 1980: 43 (own translation of the quote).

IV. The New Civil Society Places – Refuges for Children in Need

Civil society initiatives: an overview

Dealing with the topic of »OVC« in Namibia, one may be tempted to write this as a history of misery, a history of escalating crisis. The results of our research project make it clear that this would be correct and appropriate, but that in doing so one would overlook a decisive component. In the regions we examined, there is an overwhelming number of initiatives, which are almost exclusively run by – mostly older – Namibian women. It is not rare at all for these to be one-woman-initiatives, most of which were founded from the 1990s onwards in the wake of the HIV/AIDS epidemic. Usually, the initiatives are dependent on donations, which are often given by European or North American sources. These initiatives include anything from informal institutions to officially recognised state-controlled institutions, organisations, and programmes. A few examples:

- The *Namibia Children's Home* (NCH) in Windhoek (in the Eros district) is the only public children's home with capacities for about 140 children. It is subject to the authority of the *Ministry of Gender Equality and Child Welfare* (MGECW).
- *SOS Children's Villages* exist in Windhoek, Ondangwa, and Tsumeb.[162]

---

162 See the website https://www.soschildrensvillages.ca/namibia/sos-childrens-village-ondangwa.

- The *Hope Village Children's Home* – a long-term institution in Katutura – has capacities for about 90 children and adolescents from infancy up until adulthood.[163] The institution was founded in 2004 by pastor Mariejtie de Klerk.
- In 1999, former member of parliament Rosa Namises started taking in children in her house in Katutura. Today, an average of 15 children and youths live in her *Dolam Children's Home* – many of them on a permanent basis. They are orphans and children who, due to extreme poverty, cannot be raised by their families; some children have also had experiences with domestic violence and were brought to the home by the *Women and Child Protection Unit* (a police station within the Katutura state hospital). The supporting organisation of the children's home is the *Dolam Children's Home Trust* – a registered charity organisation.[164]
- The *Megameno Children's Home* was founded in 1989 by Maria Teresia. The institution takes care of around 30 OVC and was officially registered as a children's home in 2002. Megameno's manager is Risto Ashikoto, a friend of the Shaalukeni family.
- At the *Orlindi Place of Safety* – a government-registered temporary home in Katutura – around 30 children between infant age to adolescence receive support. The institution was founded in 1995 by Claudia Namises.
- The *Genade Kinderbewaarhuis – Place of Safety* in Katutura is a temporary home for OVC with an integrated preschool kindergarten. The initiative looks after about 40 children. Half of those live in the in-

163 See the »Ombudsmann Namibia Annual Report 2018« on pages 31–35: https://www.ombudsman.org.na/wp-content/uploads/2019/09/2018-report.pdf.

164 See the website of the German charity organisation »Pallium – Forschung und Hilfe für soziale Projekte e. V.«: www.pallium-ev.com (in which the authors of this book are engaged).

stitution, the other half goes to the kindergarten.[165] The house was founded in 1988 and is being managed by Justine Stephanus.

- *Walvis Bay Kid's Haven* was founded in 2008 by Maureen Baard. At the institution in Walvis Bay roughly 30 OVC have found a home. Among the Haven's supporting institutions is, for example, the local NGO »Promiseland«.
- 18 children between the ages of 3 to 16 years live at *Clara's Children Home* in Groot Aub (a village about 55 kilometres from Windhoek).[166]
- The *Home of Good Hope* in Katutura was founded in 2007 by Namibian Monica Imanga together with Eileen Greene, a nurse from Canada. Around 800 OVC benefit from the project, which provides daily meals for children. In addition to the soup kitchen, the *Home of Good Hope* helps children pay for school uniforms and covers other school-related expenses (like school supplies, transportation costs, or paraffin for candles to make studying at home easier). (Preventive) health care is also part of the programme. The NGO has also firmly established a regular influx of volunteer workers from Canada and other countries.[167]
- The project *Family of Hope Services* supports more than 400 children and youths in Katutura. It was founded in 2003 by Namibian Abigail Bachopi. Today she is the project director. Meanwhile, Foibe Silvanus acts as the project's manager. More than 270 children benefit from Family of Hope's soup kitchen. Vegetables are grown at a garden on the project premises. Additional services rendered by the project include counselling and play therapy by social workers, a playground for children, an educational programme for dropouts as well as for children and youths who never went to a school. The educational programmes are aimed particularly at children and

---

165 See the website of the Italian NGO »Happydu«: https://www.happydu.org/gena-de-e.html; and see: Namibian Institute for Democracy 2018: 23.

166 Ibid.

167 See the website of »Home of Good Hope«: https://homeofgoodhope.ngo/nutritional-initiatives.

youths who struggle with learning (due to sickness, malnutrition, or trauma). A bicycle workshop at the project generates revenue and serves as a training institution. There are also a kindergarten and a preschool.[168]

- At the *Havana Soup Kitchen* over 40 OVC at preschool age receive breakfast, lunch, and preschool teaching Mondays to Fridays. Only few of the children live with their biological parents. The project is headed by Frieda Kemuiko-Geises who founded the initiative in 2010. Aside from food and education, Christian upbringing is also an important aspect of Frieda's work. She wants to convey to the children that their lives have meaning. The soup kitchen also includes a family aid programme, where households in need receive support fulfilling basic needs (this mainly targets grandmothers who take care of many OVC). Since 2011, the project has received regular help from Volunta volunteers (German Red Cross).[169]

- *Beautiful Kidz Namibia* is a Christian interchurch organisation. Since 2003, the project has helped OVC at their own day care in Katutura. Since 2014, the project has also run a day care centre in Ovitoto (Otjozondjupa region).[170]

- The charity organisation *Oonte OVC* in Ondangwa manages a day care centre for approximately 650 children and youths who can come there three afternoons per week to receive a meal, play, and study for school. Vegetables are grown for self-supply and sale; a fishpond and a pigpen are kept to the same end. The centre also runs a bottle recycling project, computer courses, life skills courses; children receiving clothing, school uniforms, school supplies, and Oonte pays for school accommodation (the hostel), as well as

---

168 See the website of »Family of Hope Services«: https://www.familyofhopeservices.org/what-we-do/.

169 See the website of the German charity organisation »Pallium-Forschung und Hilfe für soziale Projekte e. V.«: www.pallium-ev.com.

170 See the website of »Beautifulkidznamibia«: https://www.beautifulkidznamibia.nl/de/over/.

covers additional school-related expenses. Oonte's support aims at the areas of: 1) education and training, 2) psychosocial support, 3) nutrition, and 4) health. Oonte was founded in 2004 by Petrine Shiimi who leads the organisation until the present.

- At the *TOV Multipurpose Center* in Tsumeb, pastor Edward Amadhila takes care of OVC from the San people, who are particularly disadvantaged in Namibia. The centre includes a farming project, life skills courses, a soup kitchen; children receive clothing, school uniforms, school supplies, and the TOV covers additional school-related expenses.
- The *Witvlei Foster Home* in Witvlei, in the Omaheke region, is not an officially registered institution. The informal initiative takes care of a relatively small number of children. Due to a lack of donations its future was uncertain in 2018.[171]
- The *Bright Future after School Program* of the Sam Nujoma Multipurpose Center (Ongwediva Town Council) offers a variety of services for OVC in Ongwediva and the surrounding villages (help with homework, soup kitchen, musical, artistic, and sports activities, knitting and sowing courses, computer courses, psychological counselling, life skills courses etc.).
- The *Okashomba OVC Centre* is an afternoon centre for more than 70 OVC who receive help with their homework and can participate in gardening activities. Located in the northern Oshana region (in the Okaku constituency), the initiative was founded by youth activist Albertina Shilikomwenyo.[172]
- The label OVC also includes children with disabilities. For them, there are the following initiatives in Windhoek: the *Moreson Special School*, the *Dagbreek School*, the *Onyose Trust*, the *Side by Side Early Intervention Centre*, *CLaSH – Language, Speech and Hearing impairments*, and the *Human Dreams e. V. Project;* in Walvis Bay: the *Walvis*

171   See the »Ombudsmann Namibia Annual Report 2018« on pages 31–35: https://www.ombudsman.org.na/wp-content/uploads/2019/09/2018-report.pdf.

172   Oshana Regional Council 2018: 16 et seq.

Bay Child and Family Centre; in Rehobot: the *Lebensschule Rehoboth*; in Swakopmund: *C.H.A.I.N – Children with Handycap Actions in Namibia*; in Oshakati: the *Dr. Aupa Frans Indongo Special Care* Centre; in Katima Mulilo: the *Cheshire Home* and the *Mainstream Foundation*. The national NGOs dedicated to helping children with disabilities include the *Namibia Association of Children with Disabilities* (NACD) and the *Autism Association of Namibia*.

- The emergency shelter *Friendly Haven – Place of Safety* in Windhoek offers shelter and refuge for women and children who have experienced violence or are threatened with violence.

Further examples of initiatives can be found in the »Guide to Civil Society in Namibia 2018«.[173]

The stationary institutions for OVC, the so-called *residential child care facilities* (RCCF), include 1) *children's homes* (long term institutions), 2) *places of safety* (temporary institutions), and 3) *shelters* (open, temporary institutions, primarily for street children). According to the most recent available statistics, nationwide there are 42 RCCFs with over 1,000 OVC each. More than half of these institutions can be found in the urban Khomas region and in the, also central Namibian, Erongo region.[174]

Within the framework of the research programme[175] on which this book is based, we conducted interviews with initiatives for OVC (CSOs: Civil Society Organisations) and in stationary institutions for OVC (RCCFs) and used participant observation methods. This has made it possible to trace the patchwork of informal and formal, small and large, spontaneous and long-term initiatives.

---

173 Namibian Institute for Democracy 2018; see also p. 20 of the following report by the Ministry of Gender Equality and Child Welfare: http://www.mgecw.gov.na/documents/560522/565816/Annual+Report+2012+2013.pdf/96296c0d-44ab-4bfb-8914-283a364ef0c9?version=1.0; and the directory of the Legal Assistance Centre 2005.

174 UNICEF 2020: 44.

175 See the project description at the end of this book.

Nearly all of the initiatives are in financially precarious situations. With the exception of the *Namibia Children's Home* (NCH) none of them are government-funded, but they are all subject to increasingly control by the government and its standardisation ambitions. The Ministry of Gender Equality and Child Welfare, which is responsible for OVC, wishes to formalise the initiatives more strongly. Currently, it is mostly the officially registered institutions that work closely with the authorities. Children are referred to children's homes via court order by the ministry. This state control is missing in informal homes. At times, there are cases where the latter cannot provide information about the origins of their children. This lack of transparency arouses suspicion by the authorities – also in terms of how donations are put to use. On the other hand, informal institutions can react to emergencies in a less bureaucratic immediate way and take in children even when there are no court orders to that effect.

Many of the institutions have founded their own welfare organisations to serve as supporting organisations. The *welfare organisations* include *community-based organisations* (CBOs), *faith-based organisations* (FBOs), and *non-governmental organisations* (NGOs). The help that these render includes providing homes/shelter, soup kitchens, kindergartens/preschools, medical support, day care, sports and leisure time activities (*kids clubs, day care-* and *after school centres*), counselling, material, social, and psychological support, as well as a nationwide telephone hotline (*LifelineChildline*). Among the largest organisations are *LifelineChildline, Catholic AIDS Action* (CAA), and the *Namibia Red Cross Society* (NRCS). Major umbrella organisations are the *Namibia Network of AIDS Service Organizations* (NANASO) and the *Church Alliance for Orphans* (CAFO).

Many of the smaller initiatives do not view themselves under the label »civil society«. De facto, they are an important safety net, practically a link between government institutions and eroding families. Against the background of the large gap between state and family, both of whom fail in their own ways, they fulfil the tasks of a civil society emergency institution. The motivations of their supporters range from immediate humanitarianism and religious impulses to the search for a task that is purposeful while also enabling a modest existence. The structure of the initiatives is often highly informal which leads to tensions and conflicts with foreign donors. The initiatives often live from hand to mouth, using a type of mixed financing made up of some subsistence, foreign donations, and local contributions (mostly maize, but also fruits or leftover meat from butchers, sometimes also game from commercial hunting lodges). The model for these initiatives seems rather reminiscent of the rural *egumbo*, the farmstead in northern Namibia where women are responsible for the welfare of children. They, i.e. the women, maintain traditional sociality by traditional means, which are tailored to having many children and limited resources. The women who, traditionally, are closely connected to childcare, who are confronted with children in extremely difficult circumstances, they have to »muddle through«: between the controlling state and controlling donors, constantly occupied with questions of survival, something takes shape bearing the contours of a societal »inbetween«. The initiatives are framed by the forming state which is not yet a welfare state and may perhaps never become one; by the eroding family which is the old refuge but showing more and more cracks. The erosion of the family threatens the traditional central form of social security in Namibia. The disempowerment of traditional forms of social security coupled with the simultaneous widening of social gaps in Namibia creates a situation in which the OVC initiatives become a crucial element of bottom up social innovation.

There is a growing number of people who fall out of subsistent rural worlds and feel exposed to a market-oriented life world, which do not feel they can measure up to. It appears reasonable to therefore claim that the delicate initiatives, which form a fragile safety net for OVC are rather important. They carry the torch of the traditional egumbo, while at the same time something like a civil society initiative stirs within them.

Unlike in industrialised contexts, the initiatives' supporters are usually not tied to civil society discourses, which are only now burgeoning in Namibia. Their initiatives are not rooted in civil society but in humanitarian pragmaticism. By no means do they dismiss traditional agrarian lifeworlds lock, stock, and barrel, but they connect to them – drawing on the supermarket modernity wherever it is necessary and possible. It is not uncommon for these institutions to branch into agriculture or even cattle breeding. It may be said that these initiatives make considerable contributions to humanising the daily life in Namibia and towards creating cohesion within a modernising society.

What follows is a description of some of these initiatives.

Lucia: a lively woman and her fosterlings[176]

How many strokes of fate can a person bear? How many upheavals can a life endure? Lucia's biography reflects the recent history of Namibia: apartheid, liberation war, torture, hunger, then the independence of Namibia, the outbreak of the HIV/AIDS epidemic. Later, the deaths of her son who had returned from the GDR and her sister due to AIDS. During her work as an AIDS counsellor at a hospital Lucia saw (today, she is retired) many children, young men, and women die.

»I must help people. God created me this way,« said Lucia when she was 64 years old, shortly before her retirement. And we will tell her life's story here (in parts) because it is astonishing. So many strokes of fate. Yet this chain of calamities did not leave her bitter, did not make her a misanthrope, but a person full of empathy, which shows particularly in her dedication to children. The struggles surrounding political liberation and her own survival did not break her or tire her out. Being near her feels like sitting next to a volcano that could jump to action at any moment. She can be loving, aggressive, peaceful, fierce, in a good or a foul mood, respectful and disrespectful, she may be despondent, dictatorial, and empathetic: But most of all, she can laugh – her booming laughter both infectious and irresistible. She can cry with those

---

176 Most of the names in this chapter have been changed.

who cry. She eats whatever is available, she is proud and pragmatic at the same time. She kneels before her Queen, but audaciously drags twenty German students into the festival tent of a wedding party so that they may eat from the buffet. The thought occurs that in her the whole vitality and fortitude of Namibian women – who today in many places make life more bearable and see to it that children have something to eat – coalesces.

That said, it is probably best to try and tell something about this life which up until today radiates immense power, a power which neither upheavals nor calamities could grind down. Lucia has lived through the offshoots of missionary history, colonial history, civil war, independence, and development aid industry and she has tried to weather all these storms. Compared to the official written history, the biography is a piece of lived history from the bottom. Time and again she had run-ins with grand politics, but Lucia is a guerrilla warrior of the daily life. A patchwork of resistance, humanity, and the upholding of personal and familial interests.

In 1977, Lucia was 25 years old. At the time, she was an assistant nurse in Windhoek. On April 15, 1977, she was arrested by Captain N. of the Security Branch of the South African police. The reason, she was told, was that she was a »friend of a terrorist«.[177] Lucia was pregnant at the time. She was taken to the central police station in Windhoek and, a few days later, transported several hundred kilometres north to Oshakati. In the office rooms of the Security Police she was interrogated by Black police officers. Because she could not answer the questions, which she was asked they threatened to take her to a place where they made people talk. Then she was blindfolded and escorted to another room in the same building.

»There were a number of people in the room and I gathered that they were White. Joseph (the Black policeman who had interrogated her)

---

177   Human Rights Watch 1993: 52 et seq.

put a block of ice in my mouth and a piece of cloth was firmly tied around my mouth so that I was unable to open it.

I was then suspended by my arms with my back against a wall and my arms above my head, tied individually to some object in such a manner that my feet were completely clear of the ground, and my full weight was carried by my wrists, which I subsequently ascertained had been tied to bars above the windows by two towels.

The White people then questioned me, using Joseph as an interpreter. I answered those questions which I could, but many questions were put to me which I was unable to answer.

After my interrogation had continued for some time, I suddenly felt terrible pain and shaking and trembling across one side of my face and my whole body on that side but was not aware of what caused this. This lasted for a period, which I estimate to be between one and two minutes and then suddenly stopped, whereupon I was told that if I did not talk I would be killed. I answered all the questions, which were put to me in the affirmative as I did not wish to be subjected to further treatment of this nature, even though my answers were untrue. The people interrogating me told me that they were not satisfied, and I experienced the same pain and trembling and shaking as previously, but this time on the other side of my face and body.«

When Lucia was returned to her cell at the Security Police station, she noticed that she had serious vaginal bleeding. The floor of her cell was covered in blood. When she called for a doctor, a man in uniform who claimed to be a doctor came and examined her. He said she had an infection and prescribed aspirin and antibiotics. A few days later she was interrogated by a White officer named V. N. who punched her square across the face when he was not satisfied with her answers. She finally made a statement for him. On May 10, 1977, a colonel came to her and told her she was free, she could leave. She was not sentenced to anything. But she had to cover the 480 kilometres back from Oshakati to Windhoek on her own. The bleedings that had started after the first interrogation continued for fifteen days. The electrical shocks had caused a miscarriage. Afterwards, her menstruation remained unsteady and she had to receive ongoing medical care.[178]

Thirty-five years later, once again in northern Namibia, and also close to Oshakati. Lucia visits a child headed household. This sounds bureaucratically cool: Hidden beneath it are children who keep their own household. Especially due to the effects of the HIV/AIDS epidemic, this has become not an uncommon phenomenon in Southern Africa. If parents died to AIDS; if parents work thousands of kilometres away; if they do not care because they disappeared into another family: In all of these cases, children have to take care of themselves. Hendrina, wearing a white shirt and a grey skirt, is 17 years old. Together with her 8-years-old brother David (both of their names have been changed here) she lives in an *egumbo* in northern Namibia. The small boy is wearing a violet short-sleeved shirt, part of his school uniform, and black pants. Since the death of their grandmother, the two have been living on their own. Their mother lives in Windhoek. The children are not in contact with her. As for the father: »He is nowhere to be found«. David goes to the village school. Hendrina does too. Although she is hearing-impaired due to a disease and should go to a special school which does not exist in her village. But the teacher in her village does not want girls to be alone during the day. And there is also the fact that she receives a meal of maize porridge each day at school. The siblings earn a couple of dollar by doing odd jobs for their neighbours.

The *egumbo* of Hendrina and David is a weak callback to the *egumbo* tradition. Half of the fence is decayed, some of is not even made of stakes but thin bamboo sticks plunged into the sand. Apart from a few chickens there are no animals, the cooking place seems abandoned. Rubbish and three rusty wheel rims serve as seats and saucers to keep the pot steady atop the fireplace. Sometimes female neighbours cook for the children, too.

Inside of the shack there are two beds for the children. A couple of chickens are hiding beneath them because – according to Hendri-

---

178   Ibid.

na – they are scared of zebra spitting cobras, which, indeed, are very dangerous and venomous. Then again, chickens seem to be the very thing that attracts these snakes and so they are chased out of the hut.

On the beds there are dusty wool blankets, the few pieces of clothing are strewn across the room, on a small tin table are the children's handful of possessions, and on the floor: rubbish, a beaten shoe, plastic pieces, balls of paper, wrinkled exercise books.

This is Lucia's cue: There is no broom, but without hesitation she grabs a stick that is lying in the vicinity and starts to »sweep« the hut. Bent over, she gathers all of the refuse, then pulls and shoves it out of the hut. Afterwards, she takes the dirty, dusty wool blankets and carries them outside to her car. She will wash all of them overnight – the Namibian Red Cross had brought new blankets for both of the children. Lucia worries about the young unprotected girl. She is pretty, alone a lot, nearly deaf – a potential future rape victim. Lucia would like to see her moved to an SOS Children's Village; however, the girl is too old to be accepted there.

Lucia curses, Lucia laughs, Lucia cries, Lucia, in passing, does whatever she can for these children with whom she essentially has no connection, whom she just met. Nothing links her to the children, except that they are abandoned and helpless.

From the torture, she had to endure until today: Lucia experienced the history of the liberation war in Namibia just as much as she did the AIDS catastrophe – she was an HIV/AIDS counsellor at a hospital. During her life, every imaginable thing has happened: Her cousin was shot during a massacre; she gave birth to a severely disabled child whose father was White, a British doctor – a crime during Apartheid. She was arrested and tortured. During the liberation war, she crouched through the Angolan bush. She sent her three-year-old son to the GDR to keep him safe him from the fighting: He passed away as a young man, returning from Germany to a liberated Namibia only to contract HIV and die of AIDS. Her sister, mayor of a town in northern Namibia, died to AIDS; as did her brother-in-law, friends, colleagues. One of her brothers committed suicide. She visited relatives who – like Nelson Mandela – had been

A child headed household in northern Namibia: Since the death of their grandmother Hendrina and her brother David live by themselves.

incarcerated at Robben Island. Always her fate is interconnected with the public dramas. When the liberation war was over, the great epidemic started ravaging the land: As an AIDS nurse she sat in her ramshackle office at the hospital and spelled out the death sentence to her clients: »You are positive.« She suffered with her clients. Behind her in the skewed shelf the thick dusty folders with test results. She cried with them, consoled them, warned them, sent them home. Back then, before the times of antiretroviral drugs, she gruffly and clearly declared: »There is no cure«. Clarity – but never without compassion.

Talking about Lucia: that is to attempt to retrace the life's story of a fascinating woman, marred by tragic events, which never managed to break her will to live and act. The retelling cannot be but a distant echo.

»We are fighting« – is what she says time and again. Against apartheid, for AIDS orphans. Against societal and private catastrophes. The violence, strokes of fate, apartheid, torture – neither managed to break Lucia, to embitter her or make her hard: She cares for her two sons who survived. She cares about AIDS orphans – and always there are some (young) people at her home who eat there, cook, wash, sleep. She laughs about the man with the huge tooth gap (»I never saw a gap like this«) who we see by chance from our parked car. She cries, she has her fosterlings, she chaotically and consequently cares for her favourite clients: old women, albinos covered in wounds, men consumed by herpes, paralysed women, spastic children.

The bushman

In November 2003, Lucia works at a hospital in northern Namibia. She leads us to a patient room where there are six beds on each side. Each bed is occupied. On one of them, next to the corner of the room, sits an ancient bare-chested bushman. His wrinkled toothless face smiles at us, the visitors. He tugs a ball pen into his crippled hands. He writes almost incessantly on grey lined paper. To whom does he write? What does he write? Lucia says he has lived in this bed for fifteen years. He had already been there when she started working at this hospital. He seems to have decided that this bed is his residency. In our country, the flat-rate payment would have long since ended such a permanent hospital existence. Essentially, what we have here is a hidden type of care place, which the hospital management tolerates. Otherwise, what would happen to him? His people are gone. And so, he leads a life here – contrary to our image of the life of the San, the bushmen – as a seden- tary writer. Nobody reads what he writes. His possessions amount to the bundle propped up on the window recess. There is also a plastic bowl there. A bedpan lies beneath the bed, the faint smell of urine wafting from it.

Eight years later Lucia will tell us of his passing. His papers, full of text to the brim, disappeared with him. Was what he wrote down nonsense? Was it maybe great? We will never know.

Lucia's plot and her egumbo

In Ondangwa there is a gold-rush atmosphere. The city is virtually booming just like the nearby Oshakati. Both cities – and Ongwediva tucked between them – are merging. Linking them is an increasingly clogged asphalt road that is only crossed by cows and goats. The bush begins just a few metres to the left and right of the road. Bottle stores made of corrugated iron line the road on both sides but are slowly re- placed by the mostly one-floor concrete buildings in which supermar- kets, banks, and malls dwell, occasionally interrupted by gas stations, fast food restaurants, garages, pharmacies. The old informal markets with their local products where one could purchase everything from seeds to traditional beer, from hoes to beds, can hardly stay competi- tive in the long run – not while they are walled in by their competitors in Shoprite, Pep, or whatever their names may be.

Lucia acquired her plot a long time ago, leased for 99 years – as is usual here. Back then no one could foresee that this area would become the middle of a commercial district. She is surrounded by a big gas station, a hotel, a hardware store, a supermarket. Her plot is sought after, it is big and could be profitable. But Lucia does not want to part with it. The plot is supposed to be kept for her two sons. Her simple home seems more and more like a relic, surrounded by all of these modern things. She lets two rooms on a lease, three bottle stores stand on her plot, which she is paying off in increments and which has become quite a lot more valuable in the meantime. From time to time cows invade the premises and are promptly chased out by Lucia's cries and stick whacking. The cows and the black market (which is what Lucia calls the informal market) are sprinklings of the old within the rapidly modernising business area. At Lucia's, cooking is still done at a fireplace between rocks, there is one water tap for everything, papaya trees and banana plants grow here – and there are always people on the premises who hope for something, who receive something to eat in exchange for rendering small services. And always there are children, from the neighbourhood, from the rural *egumbo*, from relatives and friends.

Lucia also owns an *egumbo* some way north of Ondangwa. She purchased it a long time ago for a modest sum. A young couple lives there and tends to the huts and millet fields. In 2003, there is a young girl there who mashes the millet in the old-fashioned way. A carefully shaped hole in the ground takes in all of the millet and then a wooden masher is used to grind it down. The masher is taller than the girl. She lifts it in a swinging motion. Starting from her toes, in a flexible, explosive, dance-like move she jumps up like a spring only to bring it crashing down into the hole where the millet lies waiting. With her bare feet she shoves anything that spilled out back into the hole. At this sight, Lucia's childhood and youth come to life:

»When I was a child, we had to help our mother on the field, we also had to mash millet, we had to cook for our family living in the egumbo. [...]. At the time, we owned cows and goats. We needed *omahangu* [millet] and *oshikundu* [traditional beer] every day. We made it from millet corn and mixed it with Kafferkorn [sorghum, Lucia calls it ›Kafferkorn‹]. We also ate fruits and Lucia names: *eshe, omauila, omambibo, omatialala, okadongodongo, omakokofi, omauni* [Lucia calls them ›oranges‹], *omapukaka, efimba*.«

The San – bushmen, as Lucia calls them – have a particular love for *omambibo*: »If you are thirsty, you can dig up *omambibo*, open the fruit, and eat it. The fruit contains a lot of water.«

Lucia remembers all of this because when she was a 16-year-old girl she did not go to school. She instead helped keep the household and watched the cattle together with her brother (who would later die in the fight for liberation).

Lucia makes her living by renting out the two rooms in her stone house in Ondangwa. She additionally receives a small rent from the neighbouring bottle store since she owns the building, which it is in. She also receives a small retirement pension thanks to her former job as an AIDS counsellor. The small government-funded pension she receives is not even enough to cover the taxes for her plot. She gets *mahangu* (millet) from the *egumbo*, which she leases out. The *egumbo* of her dead father is run by a young man who was hired by Lucia. *Mahangu* is also harvested there.

Lucia's daughter C.

C. is Lucia's firstborn child. Her father is a British doctor. He knows of his daughter but has never cared for her. C. is severely disabled: both physically and mentally. Born approximately in 1969, she sits in her chair throughout the day, rocking back and forth. Frequently, she raises a flannel to her face to wipe off saliva dripping from her mouth. She often sits in the sun, gets sunburnt because she has fairer skin. Lucia always puts sun lotion on her. She laughs and at best knows a couple of words (*iyalo – thanks* ...). She is happy when visitors come by. For years she lived on Lucia's plot. Today she lives on the farmstead of Lucia's mother and her sister in the bush. On Lucia's plot she had had a traumatic experience. C. was sitting alone in front of the house. The street that runs across here comes from Oshikango, the border town next to Angola. There is a lot of lorry traffic on it. Presumably, one lorry driver stopped at the bottle store, saw C. and – hard as it may be to believe – tried to rape her. After that she hardly dared to leave her room in the house.

It took a long time until C. had learned to walk. Her grandmother carried her on her back when South African soldiers burned down the church and huts. With C. strapped to her back, the grandmother fled to Angola. There, they crawled through the bush and it was »bushmen«, as Lucia tells it, who through magic, massage, and healing herbs made it so that at some point C. could walk.

Today she shares a room with her grandmother. A burly caretaker looks after both of them. There is obvious affection and love between the ancient grandmother and her grandchild. C. lives her life free of therapies, of rehabilitation – simply being the way she is. Neither Lucia nor her mother give the impression that they would have liked C. to be any different than she is. She is the way she is and everyone in the family will take care of her when her grandmother or mother passes away.

Abandoned children: Agatha and the Baby Haven

The first encounter with Agatha in 2003 is unforgettable: heavy weighted and plagued by arthrosis, the at that time 58-years-old woman sits on a bank in a small stone house in Katutura, surrounded by children and carrying an infant on her arm. She named the house Baby Haven.

The Baby Haven was founded by Agatha in 2003. It was supposed to be a place where HIV-positive mothers could bring their children after birth. This was done because at the time many of the sick and weakened mothers would sometimes simply abandon their babies at the hospital or their extended families would sometimes refuse to take in the potentially infected children – or the families themselves might have been decimated or affected by the epidemic. With the help of donations from Germany, Agatha was able to purchase and expand the building where she takes care of the children. The running costs of the small institution with just 12 spots for children were for many years (until 2015) also covered by donations from Germany.

The Baby Haven is a reflection of Namibia's ethnic diversity: Herero, Damara, Nama, Ovambo … The adults meanwhile belong to an originally South African ethnic group (the Xhosa). The children are spoken to sometimes in Afrikaans, in Oshiwambo, English, isiXhosa. This means that they grow up according to Namibian traditions where it is natural to learn multiple languages (without school education!) since this is considered to be an aspect of everyday life. Another thing that is treated as normal is that there are multiple, as we would say, attachment figures. In that regard, life at the Baby Haven is essentially similar to regular family life.

A regular day at the Baby Haven may sometimes seem chaotic and inscrutable to our (European) eyes – but it works. From time to time German volunteers criticise that babies lie in bed too much and that there are no support programmes. But eventually someone does take them out the bed.

Occasionally, it happens that children are brought to the Baby Haven in critical condition and die there. Especially in the early days when life-prolonging medication was not comprehensively available, the Baby Haven was more of a children's hospice.

To care for dying children: For Agatha, this is part of her job, part of her reality, whereas to some of the volunteers from Germany, who are used to good medical care, it is a barely acceptable fact.

Sometimes there are disagreements on questions of health(-care) between Agatha and the volunteers. Agatha says: »We cannot take every child that coughs to the hospital. And there is no physician who comes to our place either.« She finds that many volunteers lack understanding of the fact that living conditions in Namibia are different than in Germany. One time, she complains to us – and her tone becomes caustic: »They are so full of emotions!«. To illustrate this, she puffs up her cheeks, then noisily pushes the air out of them with her fingers.

»We can learn much from Western culture – but if we were to adopt it we'd be lost,« says Agatha. She views the German volunteers who come here to help at the Baby Haven as role models for young people in Katutura: They have plans, they undergo job training, they care for their future. The difficulties in finding a job that our students may face seem, understandably so, minor issues to her compared to those of young people in Katutura who sit in front of their huts doing nothing (unable to do anything). Many turn to drinking if they have the money to do so and alcoholism affects the Baby Haven inasmuch as many of the children come from families of alcoholics.

Agatha is a pious woman, needless to say considering how prayer is a much more natural part of everyday life here than in our country. »You only believe in what you see,« she tells us, »and that is why there is a lot you don't see.« Agatha invites us to a Sunday Mass at a – as we would call it – free church congregation where (which is still rare) Black and White members meet. There is a table for visitors from which cake and coffee are served after the service. It is a service with a lot of singing, with a PowerPoint presentation, which projects lyrics and images of sunsets onto the wall. In a one-woman sketch the risks of an HIV infection from infidelity are addressed.

Once a year, Balloon Day is celebrated at the Baby Haven. It is supposed to be a birthday celebration for every child at the Baby Haven. The whole neighbourhood is invited. »Many of the children do not have parents anymore and nobody knows when their birthday is,« says Agatha. There are fatcakes, baked on open fire, cakes, small presents. Everyone happily sings »happy birthday«. A small girl speaks a prayer commemorating the deceased relatives. »We love you even if you cannot be with us today.« The older children paint greetings to their parents on the air balloon outside that is supposed to fly to the sky later. That, however, does not work out: Instead of flying the balloons burst, accompanied by the children's laughter.

Agatha, who founded the Baby Haven, who has plenty of experience with educating people about HIV/AIDS, who knows her way around Havana, Wanaheda, Goreangab, Golgotha, Kilimandscharo ...

– the poorest districts of Katutura – she speaks about the failure of the Namibian government, about neighbours' prejudices: »Nobody breaks into our place because everyone is afraid of becoming infected.« And: »One time, we wanted to bake pizza and sell it. We had been gifted an oven. But who here buys pizza from a home for infected orphans?«

Agatha sits in a wheelchair. In Germany she would probably be considered a care level III patient. Here in Namibia, she uses what little means she has to run a small children's home. She teaches courses, meets with a self-aid group for HIV-positive women, which she founded, and in addition even tries to kickstart projects that are meant to generate some income for the women. Upon hearing this, one is constantly tempted to ignore the disparities at play here: The Baby Haven has two small bedrooms for the children, a small kitchen, and a larger living- and playroom. And now it is also supposed to contain some income projects. Managers of children's homes in Germany would be speechless faced with such impositions. Not to forget: The room also already serves as the bedroom for those who stay overnight at the Baby Haven so that the children are not alone. They pack away their mattresses in the morning. There is a sewing machine but there is no material – or someone who could instruct the women, for that matter. Something Agatha has already started is a project for greeting cards. With a self-deprecating laugh she tells us that those cards were awful. They would not open in the right places etc. These things do not work without the assistance of someone who can kickstart the project – from this one room which is a bedroom for personnel, a playroom for children, a meeting room for courses and events, and which is now also supposed to become a working space.

Many children have found a refuge at the Baby Haven: some for a short while, others for longer. Paula, for example. She was four weeks old when she arrived at the institution. The mother of that infant had died in her shack. She had been suffering from AIDS and tuberculosis. An older brother of Paula had already died prior to her birth. Nothing was known about the father. The seven siblings of the mother, meaning Paula's uncles and aunts, had also fallen victim to the epidemic. Under normal circumstances they would have been responsible for taking guardianship of Paula after the mother's death. But back then nobody was left anymore. So, Paula was alone with her dying mother. At some point, her mother breathed her last and Paula lay beside her. Nobody knows for how long. Eventually, a female neighbour took a look into the shack and found Paula – and took her to the Baby Haven.

We do not know what it means to this infant to have spent the first days of its life next to a mother who grew weaker by the hour. Paula, who either received a lethal admixture if she was breastfed by her mother or was bereft of this first important contact with her mother's body. We do not know what it means to lie besides the body of the mother for hours, probably crying out of hunger and yearning. We do not know if through the fog of fear and abandonment she could also feel the loneliness of her mother who herself had lost one family member after the other.

Outside, the sun shines brightly and nine children sit in front of the house and eat. Beneath a shade roof: On a blanket and on red plastic chairs sit the rest. Cecilia, one of the staff members, has filled the dishes with noodles and tomato sauce. Hands reach into the small bowls. Most children leave their forks lying where they are, either because they are too small to use them or because they feel it is more convenient to use the hands.

John was a baby when he was taken to the Baby Haven. In 2008 – when he was five years old – he received treatment for tuberculosis and as long as he would continue to do so – said the doctors – he would not be eligible for receiving antiretroviral medicine (those are drugs meant to suppress the outbreak of HIV) since those two treatments are incompatible with each other. John is HIV-positive. On the day of our visit at the Baby Haven he is taken to the Katutura hospital because he has an abscess the size of a child's fist above his hip. Not for the first time. He is lying in Kerstin's arms who will take him to the hospital. Kerstin is a German volunteer who helps at the house for a few months. John is in her arms, the corners of his mouth tugged slightly downwards – as if he already knew what was about to happen. A while ago he had a similar abscess on his head.

In any case, he basically already knows everything about life. His mother died; his brother breathed his last in a bed at the Baby Haven right next to him last year. Even though the brother was the more vigorous child of the two. John's legs are so weak that he cannot stand. He sits together with the other children on a blanket and eats with his hands from the red plastic dish. Klaudia – a woman in her fifties who cleans here every day, does laundry, changes diapers, cooks, feeds, and sometimes sleeps (for a monthly wage of 2,000 Namibia dollar, which is approximately 134 USD) – says that John's favourite food is meat. Time and again, John suffers from fevers. Sitting on the blanket on the ground, he looks at people with the gaze of a person who knows that in all likelihood he is not meant for a wholehearted child's laugh. Sometimes he smiles, if someone lifts him into their arms, and cries heartwrenchingly when he is lowered into his bed again. In those instances, he cries like the world is about to end. We, the German visitors, knew him a little and we had never heard him speak a word. Then one day – the boy had directed his penetrating gaze at us – we greeted him with a »good morning« – and were rather surprised when he, with great clarity and very severely, replied »morning«. He sometimes uses words from Afrikaans and other times English ones. Thoughts come to mind of Exupery's Petit Prince who also speaks severely about the limitedness of his life, his stay on earth – without saying anything superfluous. When the housemother lays him down to sleep, we observe how John turns his head away from her but then grabs onto her hand. Then he turns around to face her. The corners of his mouth turn slightly upwards which creates the hint of a fragile smile. Perhaps – this might indicate – life has more in store for him than death, disease, and pain?

After the Baby Haven ceased its operations, John was taken to the state-run children's home. Today he is 16 years old. He can only stay at the children's home until he turns 18. Because of his physical and mental disabilities, he will probably never be able to live an independent life. Often, he seems serious and nervous. John has no relatives whom he could go to.

Another boy – Hangula – uses a different mode of expression as his response to similar experiences. He lashes out wildly. This is likely a resonance of bad experiences he had early in his life. His parents, who had separated, abandoned him in their house. Which is where neighbours found him and took him to the Baby Haven. When he arrived, his whole body was covered with open wounds. Today his face is full of scars. Back then nobody wanted to wash him because they were all afraid of infection. Hangula likes to laugh, to be carried around, grabs the faces and into the mouths of those who carry him.

Justine is a small, slightly wild girl. A Spanish couple wanted to adopt her, but then they returned her after a short while, saying she were a »slow learner«. The prospective parents, who went back on their offer, now at least pay for Justine's preschool.

Dramatic circumstances are what leads to children being taken to the Baby Haven. The number of mothers who cannot support their children is high. Among the reasons for this are sickness and death, poverty, alcoholism, neglect, the dissolution of social connections, lack of paternal support etc. But even in those dire circumstances the old social wealth often shines through: the self-evident cultural diversity; the ability to consider oneself member of a group; the power of solidarity.

In a conversation with a German journalist Agatha reflects about European and African culture:[179]

»If you look at Africa today, you will come to realise that most of us want to live like people in the Western world do. We have abandoned our culture, our traditions, and want to follow the Western lifestyle. But what is Western culture actually? What is it that we are chasing after? Will we be satisfied if we manage to live like people in the Western world? Do we truly know Western culture? Or do we simply want to live comfortable lives? Anyway, what I truly cherish most about Western

179 From a conversation between journalist Burkhard Plemper and Agatha in early 2008.

culture and the German volunteers is this: They want to get something out of their lives. Young people here and there have things in common: They drink, go to clubs to meet people. But the volunteers do that in a measured fashion. And that is what I would wish for, for us. [...]
We cannot return to who we once were. We have lost a lot of things. We have lost our culture, our traditions. We are left alone with our destructive values – destructive especially for women and children. We have lost our culture due to Westernisation – maybe this originated from the church, religion, education; or maybe we simply stare at the luxury and comfort of the West and no longer want to be who we are.«

Agatha believes that the important thing should be to stick together. Every church could, for example, adopt an orphan and the congregation could take care of it. In that case, the child would no longer be an orphan. It would be a normal child living among the other children in the congregation.

»Just as we know it from the traditional extended family. Essentially, adoption of children is something that is rooted in our traditions. Because in the traditional African extended family it was like this: If I were to die, my children would still call my sister ›meme‹. They would never be without mother and father. In African culture there never was such a thing as orphans. But today all of this – the African extended family – has collapsed.«

In 2013 Agatha died. For some time after her passing the Baby Haven continued to be run by relatives. Agatha was a brave, fierce person, who at a very early point in time perceived the effects of the HIV/AIDS epidemic for Namibia – and who reacted to this. She began her work in cooperation with the church organisation »Catholic AIDS Action« – until she founded her own civil society initiative in the Baby Haven. A wise lone fighter, who was a harsh critic of the developments in Namibian society: She recognised the self-service mentality of the new elites. A woman who attempted to passionately resist the doom of African traditions and who possessed great empathy for orphaned and uncared for children.

Children in poverty: Frieda and the Havana Soup Kitchen

In January 2019, Frieda takes 22 new children into her soup kitchen programme. They come from the poorest families in Havana, a shanty-town in Katutura. Overall, there are now 40 children of preschool age who are taken care of and fed at her soup kitchen Mondays to Fridays. Frieda founded the project in 2010 – here in Havana where poverty is especially acute. The limited capacities of the soup kitchen force her to only accept children whose situation is particularly dire – for example when their mother cannot work due to sickness; when the child lives with a grandmother who has to care for many children etc.

Frieda says:

> »Sometimes it takes weeks for the new children to learn that they can rely on receiving two meals a day here. It is shocking to see how they fight each other over already empty cooking pots. In the beginning we have to cook large servings. Only after a while, when the children have gotten used to regular meals, we can reduce the servings to a normal size.«[180]

Every morning at the soup kitchen begins with singing together. Then comes to playing and studying. After lunch, the children go home. 5-year-old Panduleni is one of them. He lives alone in a shack. His single parent father works seven days a week and only returns home at night. A neighbour takes Panduleni to the soup kitchen each morning.

After the severe drought in 2019, many people hardly managed to harvest anything at all. The consequences of this are also noticeable in

---

180   According to Frieda Kemuiko-Geises in a personal conversation in February 2019.

the city: In earlier times, people in the poverty-stricken areas of Wind-hoek also subsisted on beans and millet that was sent to them from the rural Namibian north. This form of support by northern relatives ceased in 2020 because people in the north do not have enough to eat for themselves.

In Namibia many old women and men totter on the edge of hunger. They dwell in huts cobbled together out of cardboard or rusty corrugat-ed iron. Often, they have to care for grandchildren and orphans. Many do not receive the Namibian basic income for people past the age of 60, because they do not have identification documents. Or – if they receive the money – often nothing remains of it since it has to support an entire family. Frieda takes care of a dozen elderly people in Havana who live under poorest conditions.

Take for example Josephine. She is 76 years old and takes care of three orphans, all of them her grandchildren. Twice a month, Frieda delivers a food package to her and her grandchildren.

One day, the old woman suddenly goes blind. Frieda organises a surgery at the hospital: First one eye shall undergo surgery, then the other. Josephine worries: During her absence thieves might steal her possessions. In her hut there is nothing but a rickety wooden frame, on it a mattress with holes from which foam spills out. (Shortly there-after, Frieda will buy a new mattress, a warm blanket for winter times and a toilet seat for Josephine.) On the dusty floor stands a bucket of water, next to it a drinking mug, shoes, and a small suitcase in which Josephine perhaps keeps a few memorabilia, documents, or clothes. A neighbour agrees to watch her hut while Jorsephine is hospitalised.

The surgery is successful. Josephine is released from the hospital. She can see out of one eye again. The second surgery is scheduled for six weeks later. During this time something happens, and the news reaches Frieda: Josephine has died. At the hospitals. Relatives had taken her there after a serious fall. But Josephine did not survive her head injuries.

Frieda takes care of the children who now live on their own in the hut. The government's own social workers do not go to the township.

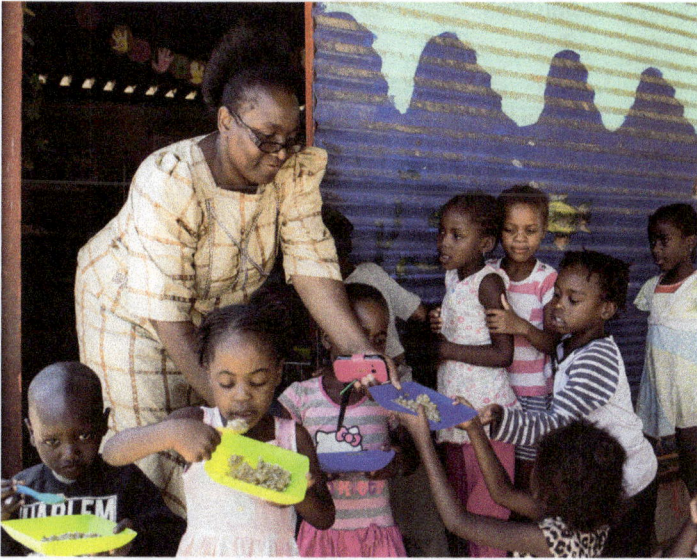

Frieda distributes lunch to the children at the Havana Soup Kitchen.

They are paid poorly, often do not own a car and thus cannot do house visits, or they do not have money for petrol.

Frieda provides the children with food, exercise books, pens, soap, and clothes. When by chance she goes by the hut two weeks later, she cannot believe her eyes: The hut has been burned down. Neighbours have piled up the burnt possessions next to the wreckage. One of Josephine's daughters sits on an upended cola box in front of it. Crying, she explains that one of Josephine's adult granddaughters had set fire to the hut in the night. She was now in police custody. This granddaughter was allegedly crazy – and dangerous. Time and again she had come to the hut and been violent towards Josephine – she wanted to steal the food that Frieda had given them. Finally, in her struggle with her grandmother, she had thrown Josephine to the ground, repeatedly bashed her head, and strangled her. Afraid of this violent woman, the family had told the hospital that Josephine had taken a fall.

Homeless children: Rosa and the Dolam Children's Home[181]

Rosa's old well-used mobile phone is broken, she urgently needs a new one. The screen of her tablet is cracked. But she pays this no mind and keeps using it. She simply ignores the spidery web of cracks. Fashionable clothing does not matter to her. She is proud of once having been voted the worst dressed member of parliament.

Visolela Rosalinda Namises was a founding member and former secretary general of the Namibian Congress of Democrats – and also used to be a member of the Namibia parliament for that party. She still wears the same clothes she wore back then: a kind of patch dress – »the typical dress that domestic servants of German settlers sewed out of the cloth scraps of dresses they made for their mistresses. For me this is still a statement [says Rosa] that we must not ever forget the colonial era.«[182]

At her Dolam Children's Home Rosa takes care of of children and youths from difficult circumstances. Her institution is almost entirely funded by donations from Germany. Up until today the 62-year-old woman works in several projects – otherwise she would be stuck with her small old age pension of 1,300 Namibia dollar (approx. 87 USD).

But even though money is constantly scarce and needed, one can feel that it holds no sway over her. She brims with vitality and the zest for life is stronger in her than the material, the worries. She tries to keep the bonds and traditions of her people, the Damara, alive. Rosa is the reigning chief of the /Khomanin people. At special locations (magic places) she communes with the ancestors. And at the children's home she dances traditional dances with the girls and boys.

Rosa represents a national opposition. Once a month she speaks on the radio. Today her pugnacious voice is known across the whole

---

181   The quotes are from different interviews with Rosa Namises, particularly an interview on September 23, 2013, at the Dolam Children's Home in Katutura.

182   Pletscher 2020.

country – especially for her fight against sexual violence, which affects Namibian women and children each day.

At the same time Rosa is a world traveller who shares her spiritual experience stemming from Damara tradition at many places across the world. She tells us of a trip to Rome, where she had been invited to a workshop. She knew she had been to St. Peter's Square but come evening she could remember nothing but the paving stones there. Shocked, she realised, she tells us, that only her body had travelled. Presentness is the most important thing. Disparity would threaten our lives. The spirit would be perched somewhere on a tree branch while the body travels somewhere else.

On the occasion of her visit to Berlin, she went to the museum of the Charité and sought out the room where at the time skulls of the Herero, and presumably also Damara and Nama, used to be kept. There, in front of the bewildered museum staff, she started dancing and chanting, spraying fragrant powders and listening to the ancestors. She spread out cloths across the room because the ancestors had complained they were naked.

In 2014 Rosa was part of the committee who received the skulls the Charité returned to Namibia and who buried them in a touching ceremony.[183]

Rosa grew up at the »old location«. She was born there in 1958. At the old location, which lay in Windhoek, people from different regional and ethnic origins lived together – as Rosa describes it. Rosa's father came from Angola. She thinks he came from a Portuguese family and a Kimbundi mother (the Kimbundu are an ethnic group in Angola). Rosa's mother is KhoiKhoi (which translates to the »true people«). The Khoikhoi and the San were the ethnic groups, which lived in the Southern African west when the first Europeans arrived. It was the Euro-

---

183 A YouTube video shows a brief excerpt from the ceremony on March 7, 2014, in Windhoek, where Rosa Namises – as representative of the Damara – played an important role: https://www.youtube.com/watch?v=nhia1UBbsoo.

peans who dubbed the KhoiKhoi »Hottentotten«, the San »Bushmen« (Bosjesmannen) – with unmistakable aims of discriminating them.

Rosa's mother speaks the Damara language that is characterised by its variety of click sounds. She was a girl when she and her family – along with everyone else – were violently evicted from the old location and forced to relocate to Katutura. At the old location – according to Rosa – people lived by a single creed: no race, no tribe, no class. In Katutura people were resettled to separate locations according to their tribes. Houses bore letters: H for Herero, O for Ovambo, D for Damara and G for mixed people (»Gemischte«). Rosa lived with her father in Katutura. They had a very close father-daughter-relation. Rosa says the sheltered childhood with her father instilled fortitude and confidence in her and that this still forms an important basis of her life.

In 1974, she becomes a health worker at the Katutura hospital as well as at the central hospital. These were apartheid times and the central hospital was reserved for White people while the Katutura Hospital was for Black people. In 1984, Rosa is fired for her political activism – and for disrespecting racial segregations. She increasingly got into conflicts with a country which as the »fifth colony of South Africa« was subjected to apartheid laws:

> »As a nurse who could not shut her mouth when White doctors and patients treat her with disdain, she gets into serious trouble. When she falls in love with a White doctor and walks hand in hand through Windhoek with him, she crosses the line. He is restationed, she is fired – and becomes a resistance fighter. For her things are clear: A system that prohibits love must be abolished. She fights against apartheid and occupation, becomes a member of SWAPO, the Namibian independence movement.«[184]

After the South African government banned the SWAPO and their gatherings, Rosa and her friends invited people to barbecue parties.

---

184   Dregger 2014 (own translation of the quote).

»Outside people were partying, while inside we'd be conspiring.«[185] On mornings, when she rode the bus to work, she distributed flyers.

Rosa is transferred to the central hospital because her superiors think it will be easier to control her there. In 1984, she is arrested for the first time because political activism was illegal. During a night shift she is called from her duties because of a flyer: »You realise this has your name on it?« »Yes, that's my name. We want to organise a *braai* [Afrikaans word for ›barbecue‹].« »You cannot do this.« Members of the intelligence service take her to the head nurse who tells her: »A nurse must not engage in political activism.« »It is just an invitation and has nothing to do with politics.« The conflicts between her and her superiors escalate. »I started to make a ruckus: ›Long live the freedom fight, long live the SWAPO!‹ [...] So, they carried me away in a car, four, five people. I was in prison for two, three months.«

After her release from prison, Rosa is once again transferred, this time to a bush clinic outside of Windhoek. During her shifts Rosa speaks in the local languages with her patients: Oshiwambo, Otjiherero, Damara, Nama – and agitates further by doing this. She learns much about the lives of farmers because most bush clinics were situated on the lands of White farm owners. Some time later Rosa is once again arrested. It is assumed that the pope at the time intervened because some of the prisoners were Catholics. Rosa is released after two weeks. Authorities try to get her diagnosed as mentally ill. Without process, she is incarcerated for 14 months. Afterwards she goes into exile to Europe and the USA. Only after the independence in 1990 does she return, ready to help build a new, free nation. But then her relations with the SWAPO degrade. Some people who return from exile are accepted by the SWAPO, others are viewed as spies. Initially, Rosa does not want to believe the reports about the SWAPO dungeons during the war. Up until then she had described herself as a firm supporter of the SWAPO and Sam Nujoma. But when her sister and friends return from

---

185 Ibid.

exile, she learns what had happened to them. Rosa enters a state of utter confusion and depression. She leaves the SWAPO.

From 1991 she works at the »Legal Assistance Center« – until 1999. At that point a new party, the »Congress of Democrats«, emerges, and she becomes a member. For five years she serves as a member of parliament.

There are many stories about her opposition and work in parliament. When the president attacked people wearing dreadlocks and uttered threats against homosexuals, Rosa immediately took to wearing dreadlocks in parliament (she still does to this day). She fights for the rights of homosexuals and for laws that penalise domestic violence, for laws that penalise rape and grant better protection for children. At the end of her time as member of parliament, she founded »Women Solidarity Namibia«, a civil society organisation that primarily deals with the issue of violence against women and children. She is also a co-founder of the women's magazine »Sister Namibia«.

Already during her time as a member of parliament, Rosa increasingly comes to realise that she cannot just sit in parliament without doing anything practical to help improve the situation for children. One day in 1999, she discovers that a girl (a playmate of her daughter) sleeps and lives in a car wreck. She takes the girl into her home. The child's mother – as it turns out – is an alcoholic and incapable of taking care of her daughter. It is experiences like this that make her found the »Dolam Children's Home«. In 2001, the civil society organisation that supports the children's home is found. Rosa's own home becomes a shelter for more and more children. This continues until in 2013, when 22 children and youths live in her small house in Katutura. When the house becomes too crammed because the children are growing up, donations from Germany help her build a new Dolam Children's Home – on a plot that Rosa had previously purchased from the Windhoek municipality at a cheap price. The new house opens in 2018. Every single child living there has their own unique story. Like the two siblings who during school vacation return home and then sleep with other siblings and their parents beneath a tree. A donkey cart serves as a bed for the family who live in the so-called »corridor«. Corridor is what people call the small strip of land between the tar road and the fenced farms. This where the landless settle, e.g. farmers who had to vacate their farms after their retirement.

At the Dolam Childen's Home on a Saturday afternoon, still at the old house: All of the children and youths have cleaned the house together. Jonathan, 16 years old, lanky, is knitting a pink scarf for himself. The girls are braiding their hair, which takes hours. Every now and then, tufts of hair are swept up and carried out. In the back, a cartoon is on the TV, but nobody is really watching. There are conflicts, but that is normal. 22 young people who essentially self-organise their lives in such a crammed space. And everyone who is here shoulders their own life's burden. Like 15-year-old Elizabeth who was raped when she was 13. Her child lives with relatives. She struggles with deciding whether she should be a mother or a child. A while ago, Rosa took Elizabeth to visit the family where her child lives. The young girl had not seen her child since its birth. Everyone sat in the room. And then Rosa pointed at the child and asked: »Do you know who that is?« Elizabeth, tears running down her face, responded: »Yes, that's my child.«

Rosa's sister lives on a farm in Okandjira, close to the city of Okahandja. The farmland is part of a former White farm estate. This is where the Dolam children spend their school holidays. The former farm workers, who now live scattered around the area, endure life as it is: miserable, poor, often teetering on the brink of hunger. They depend on occasional visitors from the city to bring them something to eat. There is no work here. Men try to earn a little bit of money with small deals like producing wood charcoal. But, in essence, one can say that here the city feeds the countryside. What is missing – is it initiative, water, competence? Thousands of hectares, yet hardly anything happens. Rosa: »Sometimes all you can do is sit down and cry.« Many of those who sit here on the sand between desiccated bushes and trees are alcoholics: »They are drinking their day away.«

In 2016 Rosa comes up with the idea of building a vegetable garden at the farm. She asks for advice and support. Water, money, and expertise are needed. One year later there is a thriving community garden in Okandjira, nearly 2000 square metres large, with a water retention basin and water tank that collect rainwater from the gutters of a greenhouse. Beneath a big shade roof, sweet potatoes, spinach, onions, carrots, melons, eggplants, tomatoes, corn, and peppers grow. Members of the farming community built the garden together with a Kenyan expert. They received coachings in vegetable cultivation, water management, and marketing. Later there was a training in organic farming by the »Namibia Organic Association«. The vegetables are used by the nine families involved in the garden, surplus is sold to neighbours and even at the organic market in Klein Windhoek.[186] Even in 2019 – during the drought – vegetables are harvested in Okandjira. The farmers feel how the fresh vegetables positively impact their health. One member of the group, an old man, is happy about having something to do again. One of the women says that the best thing for her is that they are no longer called »tombo people« (the beer drinkers). If today they go to the livestock market in Ovitoto and sell their vegetables, people there say: »See, the gardeners are coming.«

Infants and HIV-positive mothers: Mount Sinai Center

2013 at the Mount Sinai Center. More than one hundred women with babies on their arms sit on plastic chairs arrayed in rows beneath a plastic pane that shades them from the sun. They are waiting for the distribution of food and milk formula. Christaline Vega-Biart is the founder of the Mount Sinai Center in Katutura. Christaline and her team are busy packing food packages and distributing them. They know that the mothers who have come today took their ARV pills on an empty stomach and then walked between 5 to 15 kilometres on foot to reach the Center. ARV refers to antiretroviral drugs, which HIV-

---

186   Further information about the »Dolam Children's Home« and the »Okandjira Garden« are available on the website: www.pallium-ev.com.

positive people have to take in order to prevent the outbreak of AIDS. Many women collapse from exhaustion when they reach the center. Christaline and her team hurriedly distribute drinks and bread with peanut butter. The women have to take ARV pills, but these are incompatible on empty stomachs. When the women throw up the therapy is aborted – and that can be life-threatening.

Up until 2016, the Mount Sinai Center was dedicated to helping women and children from the particularly poor parts of Katutura. Children who either suffer from HIV/AIDS themselves or who are affected by the consequences of their mothers' infection with the disease. Malnutrition among the mothers causes them to produce less milk to breastfeed their children. Milk formula is used to combat this issue, but also to prevent the infection with HIV through breastfeeding.

Milk formula is expensive. The women sitting on those plastic chairs cannot afford it. The Mount Sinai Center also features a kindergarten for 20 children. A place there costs 150 Namibia dollar per month.

Christaline worked 25 years as a paediatric nurse at a public hospital in Katutura. She realised that the women and children who came to her hospital were always hungry. She began supporting the children and their mothers by filling a small cabinet at the hospital with food for especially needy mothers. When the hospital began to offer ARV treatment in 2003, Christaline was the first one to be trained in registering patient data and documenting their treatment. She also knew that infected mothers should not breastfeed their children – and she realised that she had to do something for the children. In 2005, she had the Mount Sinai Center registered as an NGO – while still feeding the children and mothers at the hospital from her store cupboard. She requested more space for her mothers' initiative at the hospital, unsuccessfully. In response, she moved her support programme to her own house in the Windhoek district of Khomasdaal. This meant that women would travel from the informal settlements of Katutura to Christaline's home to receive food and milk formula once a month. The babies were weighed and examined, all results noted down, and if there were any complications they would be taken to the hospital.

Christaline paid for all of these activities with her own salary and that of her husband who was a doctor. The church and the community contributed small sums. Her house and garage became sites for workshops, trainings, and counselling. It that was there that 30 HIV-positive women learned how to build small income-generating activities to support themselves.

In 2007, Christaline retired from her work at the hospital because the work at the Mount Sinai Center had become so massive that it could not be accomplished as a side job. Her husband used his income to take care of their household, which let Christaline focus on helping mothers and children in need. But then in 2008 her husband unexpectedly died from a heart attack. The following years were difficult for Christaline. She headed the Mount Sinai Center and took care of her own children – without an income. Finally, Christaline's dilemma was brought to the attention of politician Henk Mudge who began to support her work. The city of Windhoek granted her a large plot of land on Makkabeer Street in Katutura for free and the Spanish Embassy financed the construction of a building on that plot. In 2009, the new Mount Sinai Center celebrates its opening. The Standard Bank Namibia takes on a three-year funding for the running costs of milk formula. Several companies donate food.

The Mount Sinai Center features a small vegetable garden and a project where pearls are turned into small gifts. There is also some sewing with the mothers. At the »Katutura Soap Project« mothers learn how to make soap from olive oil.

At the time of our interview with Christaline on September 14, 2013, the Center provides 116 mothers and their children with food and hands out milk formula for 68 babies each day. It is Christaline's wish to expand the centre even further: a kitchen was needed. And a few rooms that could be leased out to generate some more income for the centre. »My dream is to see the children and babies whom we helped return later in their lives to become involved and help other children and babies.« But at the time – said Christaline – there were many other challenges. For example, supporting mothers with milk formula was difficult since the women did not have enough firewood at home to cook the milk several times a day. This led to women preparing an entire bottle for the day at once, but due to a lack of cooling opportunities the milk would get spoiled over the course of the day. And this in turn gave children diarrhoea and made them sick from drinking spoiled milk.

When the bank funding ended and no other donors were found, Christaline starts working again: as a nurse at an old age home. As soon as possible, she would however stop this to dedicate all of her attention to the Mount Sinai Center.

Christaline's attention faced many great difficulties like this time and again. On January 24, 2015, Christaline dies a sudden death. Too young and after a short hospital stay. Her son takes over duties at the Mount Sinai Center for a time. But today it no longer exists.

Unforgotten is the image of a woman with twins, carrying one on her back, the other on her arm. She left the centre carrying a heavy burden: milk formula, food. On the rows of chairs sat emaciated women, waiting to be called forth to receive what they needed just to survive. As for how these women survive now, we do not know.[187]

Excursus: On the colonial history of orphanages in Namibia

The history of orphanages in Namibia is still awaiting revision. A few clues from the early times of the first orphanages in colonial German South West Africa reveal continuities: A mixture of readiness to help and White dominance pervades history and has yet to come to an end.[188] The history of orphanages in German South West Africa begins with church politics squabbles. The visitation report of mission inspector pastor Spiecker, published in Barmen in 1907, refers to the

---

187   On the history of the »Mount Sinai Center« see also Allgemeine Zeitung Namibia 2010.

188   See e.g. Gronemeyer/Fink 2015.

mission having been run among the Herrero since 1848.[189] The report also contains comments about the role of the Rhenish Mission during the Herero revolt. Spiecker argues that cattle farms run by Germans in Herero territory will be successful. There are also plans to farm the land: »Individual farmers there [in the area around river Omaruru] have had great success cultivating potatoes, likewise vegetable and wine cultivation will, without question, be wortwhile - especially close to the river and wherever water can be found.«[190] After the Herero revolt – so Spiecker – there were many »emaciated children at Omaruru«. And he continues: »Seeing these trains of prisoners always filled me with wistfulness, especially whenever I saw the many naked, rugged shapes, most of all the small children some of whom were very miserable and seemed more skeleton than person and who even in their tender youth had had to endure life's misery to the teeth.«[191] There were many orphans as a result of the Herero revolt. In Swakopmund – according to the report – many children perished (»[...] The dying of many an orphan in Swakopmund [...]«). Clichés mix with specific experiences:

> »The Herero are fond of children like most of the indigenous. Orphaned children could always and without difficulties find foster parents who would raise them along their own children. Which is, indeed, the most natural type of care for orphans. [...] The catholic mission, however, had always had the ambition to get a hold of these orphans so as to raise them in their religion. The military authorities who had to take care of the prisoners were very forthcoming towards the catholic mission.«[192]

The military authorities decreed that one half of the orphans were to be given to catholic, the other half to the protestant mission. However, this (according to Spiecker) violated the principle of freedom of

---

189   Spiecker 1907.

190   Ibid.: 74 et seq (own translation of the quote).

191   Ibid.: 75 (own translation of the quote).

192   Ibid.: 123 (own translation of the quote).

religion. Which seems almost cynical, considering that what it meant there is not the freedom of those children but that of competing religious officials. The children were supposedly gathered by the Rhenish Mission. The catholic mission on the other hand (said Spiecker) was backed by the mighty Zentrum (referring to the Zentrumspartei, a political party in Germany at the time). And because of this half of the orphans were sent to the Catholics. »In how far [...] the catholic missionaries employed more finesse and audacity than our brothers to lay claim to the orphans – the answer I must leave open.«[193] While in the orphanage in »Otjimbingwe orphaned Herero children are taken care of, at the Augustineum in Okahandja half-White children are raised by our missionary Wilhelm Eich, praeses of the Herero mission«.[194] And Spiecker adds: For the half-White children »it is usually out of the question to leave them to be raised by their indigenous mothers if they are to receive any successful education«.[195]

193 Ibid (own translation of the quote).

194 Ibid.: 124 et seq (own translation of the quote).

195 Ibid: 126 (own translation of the quote).

Conclusion: African Children.
European Childhoods

Living in societies of plenty.
Surviving in societies of dearth

European standards – even in their politically progressive version – today are losing their global explanatory power. They are – writes Charlotte Wiedemann – no longer a »universal toolbox for explaining the world«. Following this thought leads one stumbling towards the arduous »attempt to avoid White writing«.[196]

Did we succeed at this in this book? We at least carefully paid attention to putting the voices of the people whom we spoke to in Namibia front and centre, and we let the arguments develop based on these voices. Still, this cannot be more than an attempt to overcome the terminological and intellectual narrowness of Eurocentrism. This narrowness continues to be something

> »that to us, the descendants of a culture of expansion and colonialism, is still ingrained into the deepest reaches of our subconscious. Namely the notion that White is not a skin colour but the basic form of humanity, neutral and without preconditions. Coloured are just the others, who are special, who form ethnicities, while we are general and have ethnologists«.[197]

---

196 Wiedemann 2020: 2 (own translation of the quote).
197 Ibid (own translation of the quote).

As writers, we at least have an idea that centuries of racism have had impacts on our writing, our thinking, our lives. We may be able to tell ourselves that we have arrived at a »post-White« age, yet we may not necessarily be able to genuinely believe or feel it. This book has been driven by the endeavour to listen to the voices of others. We have tried not to interpret these powerful voices but to listen to the strength of the children and women whom we dealt with.[198]

Writing about Africa, like writing about European conditions, is riddled with fundamental difficulties. Not just with the pretend-neutral language of White Europe but also – and thus surpassing all other imaginable difficulties – with the destruction of language.

As aptly put by Ivan Illich:

»For language, things are looking similar to how they look for agriculture. The trend points away from soil culture towards agribusiness. Today, soil is hardly considered an earthen part of culture any longer – instead it is turned into a garbage dump for industrial fertilizer. Traditional farming is replaced by industrial agriculture. Just like the farmer is pushed out of agriculture, so are people removed from language. Targeted language technology grows rampantly, exhausting that language in which personal convictions and poetry find their expression.«[199]

We have not set a standard; we have neither quantified nor weighed. This necessarily creates tension between us and that which today claims the label of »science«.

---

198   Cf. Gronemeyer/Fink 2016.
199   We are grateful to Franz Tutzer 2019: 46 et seq. for this reference (own translation of the quote).

How do children experience the human condition? Approaches to an overdue cultural comparison

Tanzania: The bus trip from Dar es Salaam to Songea takes nearly seventeen hours. The bus is fully occupied. Tanzanian soaps blare at full volume from the two TVs that are fixed to the ceiling of the bus. Three short breaks are scheduled for the travellers. Twice the bus stops at the side of the road. Everything has to be done quickly. Everyone runs out into the pouring rain and to the nearby bushes. There are no toilets here. During the third rest at a roadhouse people get a chance to buy something to eat. But after ten minutes the bus driver starts honking. The trip continues.

A mother with her baby sits next to us in the bus. During the entire exhausting trip, she does not speak a single word with her child (which at a guess is barely a year old). She hardly pays it attention. The child: It is completely calm and placid. It neither wails, nor cries, nor kicks, but instead lies patiently – mostly sleeping – on its mother's lap. Only occasionally do we hear a soft wail, which the mother knows how to soothe with a short loving look, a caress, and giving it the feeding bottle. We are perplexed, asking ourselves: Is this mother's behaviour towards her child not distanced? Is this mother unloving because she does not communicate with her child, does not give it a single smile and barely any attention? Or is the relation between mother and child perhaps established primarily by something other than words and glances?

Developmental psychologist Heidi Keller has analysed mother-child-interactions in a cultural comparison. She writes:

»In traditional farmer families of the non-Western world emotional control is practised from the first day of life. The lack of emotional expression is part of the socialisation strategy which relies on hierarchical bonding. Early socialising experiences have noticeable effects on the emotion regular of one-year-old children.«[200]

Again and again, we notice similar situations in Africa: A mother wordlessly washes her crying child in a bathtub.

The wordlessness of mothers when dealing with their children is striking in both situations. It is fundamentally different from the consistent attention and addressing which is dominant in the treatment of children across European or US-American societies.

And as for the seventeen-hours bus trip: Would a German mother burden her infant with something like that? Probably not. The immediate, at times arduous and uncomfortable necessities of life for adults and children are much more present in African quotidian life. In rural areas children are traditionally tasked with fetching water, gathering wood, helping in the kitchen, watching their younger siblings, helping care for the sick, feeding and herding the cattle, and so on. For many children long walks on foot to school are the norm. Especially in the midday heat and during rainy seasons, these are far certainly far from fun. And yet they offer children opportunities to mingle and for playing. The Ovahimba woman in northern Namibia of course exposes her children to the hours-long walk through sand and under the burning sun out of necessity.

Daily life in Europe has steadily become more comfortable and, fortunately, we have been able to shed many of everyday hassles. As a consequence, children in Western societies are less exposed to experiencing life at the level of fulfilling basic necessities: They are usually not involved in earning their families' livelihood. Likewise, they are less and less needed in the steadily decreasing amount of household keeping, and even if they are asked to help keep the household it is mostly for educational purposes. As a grandmother of five in the cen-

---

200   Keller 2009 (own translation of the quote).

tral German region of Hesse puts it: »Nowadays you do not even know what you are supposed to ask of the children«.[201]

Ananke is the Greek term used to refer to »necessity«. It was an indisputable thing. It simply existed. We can assume that children realise when necessities are fabricated for educational purposes. They feel it when artificial borders are erected (for example with regards to mobile phone usage). Perhaps the only persistent remaining necessity and experience with limits in Western culture is school along with its demand of performance. But unlike learning from practical life contexts, school does not teach vivid experiences.

If there are hardly any serious, purposeful tasks for children – or if well-meaning parents do not burden or entrust children with these – then there is a real danger of these children being cut off from experiencing the human condition (from the experience of that which is necessary for life, which life presupposes). Therein lies the tragedy of modern childhood among us: Children are barred from participating in the adults' life, and thus growing into adulthood is impeded.

Ironically, efforts made to spare children the seriousness and hardships of life as well as the conflicts of adults actually expose children of modern affluent societies to a particularly severe conflict: »namely the contradiction between their childhood and real life,« in the words of Michel Foucault.[202] Foucault traces the beginning of this societal development back to the 18th century: »During the 18th century, impelled by the works of Rousseau and Pestalozzi, efforts were made to create a bespoke world for children through the use of educational rules, tailored to children's development. Inadvertendly, this created an unreal, archaic, abstract milieu around children which lacked any relation to the world of adults.«[203]

---

201 To express this sentiment, the grandmother uses a dialectal expression from the central German Vogelsberg region. The original proverb is »Was man die Kinder heißen soll« and literally translates to »what to call the children (for)«.

202 Foucault 1968: 122 et seq (own translation of the quote).

203 Ibid (own translation of the quote).

From a cultural perspective, education has always been something that emerged out of the human condition. We are currently dealing with changed conditions for childhoods, with their problematic consequences and questions as to how to handle these. If we fight and destroy the human condition, education will inevitably become something artificial, something fabricated – a project. In places where boundaries in a society are no longer a given, they – if anything at all – have to be artificially erected.

Not uncommonly, the growing uncertainty in how to deal with children has led parents as well as pedagogues to engage in a phenomenon which Monika Aly has described as »caring siege«. According to Aly, parents leave their children less and less space for themselves, which has destructive effects on their development of autonomy.[204] The disappearance of the »self-evident« in dealing with children is obvious e.g. in the immense amount of attention that parents, especially those from the »educated« parts of society, dedicate to their children. The goal of this modern education project is to prepare children as best as possible for an estranged life under performance and consumer pressures. The widespread phenomenon ADHD (Attention deficit hyperactivity disorder) clearly illustrates how we measure the value of a child depending on its ability to perform.[205] Childhood becomes an investment phase into the entrepreneurial self of the adult that it will eventually become.[206] In Germany with its low birth rates, where more and more couples (often against their wishes) remain childless the concentration on the single child is growing.

What Monika Aly describes as »caring siege« is referred to by American experts with terms like *overparenting* or *helicopter parents*. Helicopter

---

204 Cf. Aly 2008 (own translation of the quote).

205 According to Dr Klaus-Dieter Grothe in a discussion group with the authors on August 13, 2012.

206 Cf. Albrecht-Heide 2008.

parents ceaselessly hover over their offspring so as to be able to intervene at any moment. And all they want is the best for their child.[207]

»Out of fear that death could take our child from us, we deprive it of life. To prevent its death, we do not actually let it live.«[208] These words were written, with remarkable foresight, in the 1930s by Polish reform pedagogue Janusz Korczak.

More and more children today grow up in an environment that is dominated by tight schedules, parental control, and omnipresent care with at times absurd dimensions. The manager of a crèche comments on this:

> »I have been doing this job for 40 years. And the trend is such that everything revolves just around the child. Like, from top to bottom. [...] You can see it here. The children are picked up by their parents. Children are not the ones who fetch their backpacks. No, their mommy fetches them. Mommy even carries the backpack of their friend Joachim. Mommy ties their shoes. Perhaps the parents do not even realise that they are needlessly taking over mundane tasks for their children. I mean, at 6 or 7 years, they are well capable of carrying their own backpacks. They can walk to school on their own. Some schools actually do promote that. They have signs at the front entrances that say: Up to here! From here on, I walk alone.«[209]

In his book »Vermächtnis – Was wir von traditionellen Gesellschaften lernen können«[210], Jared Diamond compares the treatment of children in so-called WEIRD (western, educated, industrial, rich, democratic) societies with that in traditional societies, e.g. in Papua New Guinea:

---

207   Cf. Podjavorsek 2012: 2.

208   Korczak 1967: 44 (own translation of the quote).

209   Podjavorsek 2012: 5 et seqq.

210   American original titel: The world until yesterday. What can we learn from traditional societies? (2013)

»Autonomy is valued more highly in traditional societies compared to Western society. The children of hunters and gatherers on Papua New Guinea are more adroit at talking with their parents. They are more mature, do not experience puberty crises. Why is that? Because they grow up with much greater autonomy. They have several caregivers, not just their parents.«

And he continues:

»In our society, we push children while they lie flat in their prams, and if we carry them it is always done so that they face their parents. In Papua New Guinea children are always carried on the back. That way, they see whatever the adults see. And as soon as they can walk, they move freely. They are independent, fearless. Here with us, security is the top priority – in traditional societies freedom takes that spot.«[211]

While most societies in the so-called Third World are »gerontocratic« (meaning that in them the needs of adults are prioritised over those of children, and that elderly people in particular are held in high esteem), post-industrial societies can be described as »neontocratic« (inasmuch as in them, adults are ruled according to the needs and wishes of children). That is the conclusion of childhood researcher David Lancy.[212] According to him, »neontocratic« societies do not view children as a part of the labour force that has to contribute to the community, but what is instead expected of them is that they emotionally satisfy the adults. In New York, some mothers invest up to a hundred hours and more into preparing the birthday parties of their children, as internet reports on the websites of event agencies like *birthdayparties.com* or *partypoopers.com* show.[213]

---

211 Jared Diamond quoted in: Gürtler 2012 (own translation of the quote).

212 Lancy 2008.

213 Ibid.: 25–26; 121; 77.

Another aspect that clearly illustrates the »neontocracy« of our contemporary society is that conversations between adults often become impossible as soon as children are present – which is a phenomenon that would be unthinkable in the African context. Psychologist Michael Winterhoff argues that the reason that parents in our culture increasingly submit to the needs of their children lies in a symbiotic parent-child-relation – an increasingly frequent relational disturbance between adults and children.[214] A satirical analysis of the type of modern »middle class mommies« which is widespread in »neontocratic« society is presented in Dorothea Dieckmann's book »Unter Müttern« (Among Mothers).[215]

Against the background of mounting problems and failures in socialisation efforts in society[216], it is interesting and perhaps helpful to take a look at what is so different about the treatment of children in African contexts. In Namibia – despite manifold crises – old and new forms of socialisation essentially still seem functional. Granted, looking at Namibian childhoods by no means paints an idyllic picture (violence and experiences of abuse are part of many children's everyday life), yet disturbed or maladjusted children do not seem as obviously visibly. Not even in milieus where painful experiences would lead us to expect socialisation deficits, for instance among AIDS orphans. Why is that?

The societal discourse and the treatment of children in Namibia appears devoid of the dramaticising attention that we dedicate to children. (Which is an ambivalent sentence that is not meant to advocate the lack of care for children in difficult circumstances, but rather is aimed at the helicopter parent phenomenon.) Considering the heated emotions towards children in our culture, it may be hard for us to grasp that familial bonds in African contexts are not primarily built on emotions. Children play a vital role as contributors to the physical survival of many African families: They are both part of the labour force

---

214 Cf. Winterhoff 2008.

215 Dieckmann 1993: 102.

216 Cf. Gronemeyer/ Fink 2016.

and the pension scheme, from an early age they shoulder responsibility for the community.

Meanwhile, in our society children are at one time at the centre of attention, but at the same time they are barred from any true, i.e. purposeful and responsible, participation in the community. The possibility of autonomy for children – considered a trait of the human condition – is at risk of being smothered by consumerism. For their parents they are mostly a »resource of meaning«, for society they are »human resources« needed for securing Germany's role as an economic location.

It may be that socialisation has become so difficult among us because children and youths perceive their devaluation, the paralysis and functionalisation that is forced upon them. And what is more: In a society attempting to part with the human condition children already have a hard time experiencing it. However, should we successfully abolish the human condition, in doing so we may also lose touch with life.

We have tried to show that there are two sides to the topic of »Children in Namibia«. The often dramatic, difficult living conditions, which we described are time and again contrasted by the surprising vibrancy of the children. Many of them experience that the Namibian human condition (still) unfolds social security, communality, and moral alignment in life. The *egumbo*, which we described in our text was an example of a concretisation of the human condition, where – without being idyllic – the conditions of human life assume a social shape. The human condition: It is alive and enables socialisation conditions that apparently engender remarkable resilience against crises in Namibian children. But at the same time, the human condition is in extreme jeopardy.

Appendix

The research project

This book is based on the findings of a research project conducted between 2012 and 2015 (3 years) at the department of sociology at Justus-Liebig-University Giessen, Germany. Work in the project »(AIDS-) Orphans in Southern Africa (Namibia): Social Crisis and Social Powers« was focused on the urban Khomas and the rural Oshana region in Namibia. The research, which included months-long field research stays, was funded by the German Research Foundation. In addition to a literature analysis, workshops and conferences in Germany and Namibia, we also conducted 112 interviews: most of them with adults, but some also with children and youths. Furthermore, we gathered 167 essays written by students, some of which were published in the book »Who takes care? Children of Crisis. Essays by Namibian Learners« (2013).

The interviews with were conducted at 30 civil society organizations (CSOs) as well as at 6 stationary institutions for orphans and vulnerable children (RCCFs, residential childcare facilities). At the RCCFs we conducted interviews with managers (6) and with children and youths (9). Additional interviews were held at households (50) (among those were two child headed households), with teachers (5), and with representatives of the Ministry of Gender Equality and Child Welfare (2); further interviews (8) were conducted at an urban afternoon centre for OVC, a hospital ward for orphaned babies, a hospital police station for victims of violence, with a community worker, and with a parish priest; (2) group interviews with children were conducted at a soup kitchen of the Namibian Red Cross and at an informal initiative (both in the rural north).

After the end of the research project, we, the authors of this book, informally continued these talks: within the context of our long-standing and continuous work in the charitable association »Pallium – Forschung und Hilfe für soziale Projekte e. V.« – and, among others, during a university research trip under the topic of »Children with disabilities in Namibia« in the year 2019.

Acknowledgements

We thank the German Research Foundation (Deutsche Forschungsgemeinschaft, DFG) for funding the research project on which this book is based. Only parts of the extensive interview material was addressed in this book. Further evaluative and analytical steps will follow. For their friendship and their support in our work we give special thanks to Mathias Hangala, Albertina Haufiku, Frieda Kemuiko-Geises, Visolela Rosalinda Namises, Rauna Shimbode, Toivo Shilumbu, Petrine Shiimi; also, to Agnes Tom and Christaline Vega-Biart (both of whom sadly passed away).

We are grateful to the transcript Verlag for its readiness to make this book part of its programme. Wolfgang Polkowski took on the task of creating the text layout with his usual professionalism. Anne Zulauf and Jonas Metzger gave us cordial counsel, and Inga Schüssler worked on the finalisation of the manuscript. For the cover photo, Pietro Sutera provided us with one of his wonderful pictures. The photo shows children at the Havana Soup Kitchen in Namibia. The picture of the Havana Soup Kitchen within this book was also taken by Pietro Sutera. In a previous DFG project, Matthias Rompel established crucial contacts for our research, and he accompanied the process, which this book documents as a friend and font of knowledge. And, finally, we thank Felix Andreas Wagner for his thorough translation of the German manuscript.

Bibliography

Alber, Erdmute (2013): Soziale Elternschaft im Wandel. Kindheit, Verwandtschaft und Zugehörigkeit in Westafrika. Dietrich Reimer Verlag: Berlin.

Albrecht-Heide, Astrid (2008): Gedanken zur Kindheit als Investitionsphase, in: Ästhetik & Kommunikation 39(142), S. 43–48.

Allgemeine Zeitung Namibia (2018): Statistikamt erklärt Landbesitz, 17.09.2018, von Frank Steffen. https://www.az.com.na/nachrichten/statistikamt-erklrt-landbesitz2018-09-17.

Allgemeine Zeitung Namibia (2010): Mit kleinen Schritten Großes erreichen, vom 16.06.2010. https://www.az.com.na/nachrichten/mit-kleinen-schritten-grosses-errreichen.

Aly, Monika (2008): Fürsorgliche Belagerung. Das Drama des modernen Kindes, in: Ästhetik & Kommunikation 39(142), S. 65–68.

Augé, Marc (2019): Die Zukunft der Erdbewohner. Ein Manifest. Berlin: Matthes & Seitz Verlag.

Avanessian, Armen/Moalemi, Mahan (Hg.) (2018): Ethnofuturismen. Leipzig: Merve-Verlag.

Bächtold-Stäubli, Hanns (Hg.) (1987): Brei, in: Handwörterbuch des deutschen Aberglaubens (Bd. 1). Berlin, New York: de Gruyter, Sp.1537–1549.

BBC News (2019): How Africa will be affected by Climate Change, 15.12.1019, von Richard Washington. https://www.bbc.com/news/world-africa-50726701.

Beck, Ulrich (1994): Risk society: towards an new modernity. London: SAGE Publication.

Bode, Sabine (2014): Die vergessene Generation. Stuttgart: Klett-Cotta Verlag.

Bray, Rachel (2004): Predicting the social consequences of orphanhood in South Africa, in: African Journal of AIDS Research 2(1), pp. 39–55.

Brizay, Ulrike (2011): Bewältigungsstrategien für die Waisenkrise in Tansania. Lebensweltorientierte Unterstützungsangebote für Waisen. Wiesbaden: Verlag für Sozialwissenschaften.

Brown, Jill (2013): When all the children are left behind: an exploration of fosterage of owambo orphans in Namibia, Africa, in: Vulnerable children. Global challenges in education, health, well-being, and child rights. Ed. by Deborah J. Johnson/DeBrenna LaFa Agbényiga/Robert K. Hitchcock. Zürich: Springer Verlag, pp. 185–202.

Brown, Jill (2011): Child fostering chains among ovambo families in Namibia, Southern Africa, in: Journal of Southern African Studies 37(1), pp. 155–76.

Brown, Jill (2007): Child fosterage and the developmental markers of children in Namibia, southern Africa: Implications of gender and kinship. ETD collection for University of Nebraska-Lincoln.

Canetti, Elias (1980): Die Stimmen von Marrakesch. Frankfurt a.M.: Fischer Verlag.

Césaire, Aimé (2000): Discourse on Colonialism. New York: Monthly Review Press.

Cheney, Kristen E. (2017): Crying for our elders. African orphanhood in the age of HIV and AIDS. Chicago: University of Chicago Press.

Cheney, Kristen E. (2013): Malik and his three mothers. AIDS orphans' survival strategies and how children's rights translations hinder them, in: Reconceptualizing children's rights in international development. Living rights, social justice, translations. Ed. by Karl Hanson/Olga Nieuwenhuys. Cambridge: Cambridge University Press, pp. 152–172.

Cheney, Kristen E. (2012): Seen but not heard. African orphanhood in the age of HIV/AIDS, in: African childhoods. Education, development, peacebuilding, and the youngest continent. Ed. by Marisa O. Ensor. New York: Palgrave Macmillan Publishers, pp. 95–108.

Cheney, Kristen E. (2010): Deconstructing childhood vulnerability: an introduction, in: Childhood Africa 2(1), pp. 4–7. https://repub.eur.nl/pub/22707.

Cheney, Kristen E./Rotabi, Karen Smith (2015): Addicted to orphans: how the global orphan industrial complex jeopardizes local child protection systems, in: Geographies of children and young people. Conflict, violence and peace. Ed. by Christopher Harker/Kathrin Hörschelmann/Tracey Skelton (Vol 11). Singapore: Springer Verlag, pp. 89–107.

Crivello, Gina/Chuta, Nardos (2013): Rethinking orphanhood and vulnerability in Ethiopia, in: Child protection in development. Ed. by Michael Bourdillon/William Myers. USA/Canada: Taylor & Francis, pp. 100–112.

Dahl, Bianca (2009): Left Behind? Orphaned children, humanitarian aid and the politics of kinship, culture, and caregiving during Botswana's AIDS crisis. Dissertation, University of Chicago.

Dickie, John (2008): Delizia! Die Italiener und ihre Küche. Geschichte einer Leidenschaft. Frankfurt a.M.: Fischer Verlag.

Dieckmann, Dorothea (1993): Unter Müttern. Eine Schmähschrift. Berlin: Rowohlt Verlag.

Die Presse (2014): Wo Homosexualität ein Verbrechen ist, vom 25. Februar 2014. https://www.diepresse.com/1567431/wo-homosexualitat-ein-verbrechen-ist.

Dilger, Hansjörg (2005): Migration und Mobilität im subsaharischen Afrika, in: Leben mit AIDS. Krankheit, Tod und soziale Beziehungen in Afrika. Frankfurt a.M.: Campus Verlag, S. 49–65.

Dohr, Daniela/Kumria, Philipp/Metzger, Jonas (2015): Saatgut und Sozialsystem. Gender, Monetarisierung und bäuerliche Praktiken der Ernährungssicherung in Namibia und Tansania. Münster: LIT-Verlag.

Dregger, Leila (2014): Porträt: Ich liebe die Welt!, in: Die Wochenzeitung (WOZ), Nr. 10 vom 06. März 2014. https://www.woz.ch/-4c2f.

Edwards-Jauch, Lucy (2016): Gender-based violence and masculinity in Namibia: a structuralist framing of the debate, in: Journal for Studies in Humanities and Social Sciences 5(1), pp. 49–62. http://repository.unam.edu.na/bitstream/handle/11070/1828/Edwards-Jauch_Gender_2016.pdf?sequence=1&isAllowed=y.

Eisenstein, Charles (2018): Climate. A new story. US: North Atlantic Books.

Ellis, Stephen (2011): Seasons of rains: Africa in the world. London: C Hurst & Co Publishers.

Erkkilä, Antti/Indongo, Nelago (2017): Relocation of the homestead: a customary practice in the communal areas of north-central Namibia, in: Knowledge for justice: critical perspectives from southern african-nordic research partnerships. Ed. by Tor Halvorsen and Hilde Ibsen. African Books Collective, pp. 227–240. Project MUSE: muse.jhu.edu/book/57261.

Esteva, Gustavo (1993): Entwicklung, in: Wie im Westen so auf Erden. Ein polemisches Handbuch zur Entwicklungspolitik. Hg. v. Wolfgang Sachs. Hamburg: Rowohlt Verlag, S. 89–119.

Ferguson, James (2006): Global shadows: Africa in the neoliberal world order. Durham: Duke University Press.

Fink, Michaela (2019): Hoffnung jenseits der Verschulung. Warum wir neue Räume für Imagination brauchen, in: Was wird aus der Hoffnung? Interdisziplinäre Denkanstöße für neue Formen des Miteinanders. Hg. v. Michaela Fink/Jonas Metzger/Anne Zulauf. Gießen: Psychosozial Verlag, S. 129–143.

Fink, Michaela/Gronemeyer, Reimer (2015): Zur Lebenslage von Waisen und ›vulnerable children‹ in Namibia, in: Afrikanische Kindheiten. Soziale Elternschaft und Waisenhilfe in der Subsahara. Hg. v. Michaela Fink/ Reimer Gronemeyer. Bielefeld: tanscript Verlag, S. 15–40.

Fink, Michaela/Gronemeyer, Reimer (Eds.) (2013): Who takes care? Children of crisis. Essays by Namibian learners. Windhoek: Namibia Publishing House. https://www.researchgate.net/publication/260593659_Who_Takes_Care_Children_of_Crisis_Essays_by_Namibian_Learners_Ed_by_Michaela_Fink_and_Reimer_Gronemeyer_Windhoek_Namibia_2013.

Foucault, Michel (1968): Psychologie und Geisteskrankheit. Frankfurt a.M.: Suhrkamp.

Freidus, Andrea Lee (2011): Raising Malawi's children: AIDS orphans and a politics of compassion. Dissertation, Michigan State University.

Garschagen, Teresa (2015): Rassismus-Debatte. Was ist »Critical Whiteness«? Mediendienst Integration. 12.08.2015. https://mediendienst-integration.de/artikel/was-ist-critical-whiteness.html.

Gibbons, Judith (2013): Adoption and fostering: traditional and contemporary child welfare strategies in Sub-Saharan Africa, in: Cross-cultural psychology: an africentric perspective. Ed. by Therese Tchombe/Bambe Nsamenang/Heidi Keller/Marta Fülöp. Limbe, Cameroon: Design House, pp. 191–208.

Grill, Bartholomäus (2019): Wir Herrenmenschen. Unser rassistisches Erbe: Eine Reise in die deutsche Kolonialgeschichte. München: Siedler Verlag.

Gronemeyer, Reimer/Fink, Michaela (2016): Unsere Kinder. Was sie für die Zukunft wirklich stark macht. Gütersloh: Random House/Gütersloher Verlagshaus.

Gronemeyer, Reimer/Fink, Michaela (2015): Tunnelblick der Helfer – über Spendereinfluss und VolunTourismus in afrikanischen Waiseninitiativen, in: Conditio Humana. Beiträge zum Verlust von Welt und Leib (Nr. 2: Tunnelblick). Hg. v. Reimer Gronemeyer/ Jonas Metzger/ Andrea Newerla. Gießener Elektronische Bibliothek, S. 10–20. http://geb.uni-giessen.de/geb/volltexte/2015/11285/pdf/conditiohumana_02.pdf.

Gronemeyer Reimer/Rompel, Matthias (2007): Verborgenes Afrika. Alltag jenseits von Klischees. Frankfurt a.M.: Brandes & Apsel Verlag.

Gronemeyer, Reimer (2005): So stirbt man in Afrika an AIDS. Warum westliche Gesundheitskonzepte im südlichen Afrika scheitern. Eine Streitschrift. Frankfurt a.M.: Brandes & Apsel Verlag.

Gronemeyer, Marianne (2002): Die Macht der Bedürfnisse. Darmstadt: Primus-Verlag.

Groth, Siegfried (1996): Namibische Passion. Wuppertal: Peter Hammer Verlag.

Grothe, Klaus-Dieter (2015): Kindersoldaten und AIDS-Waisen – sind traumatherapeutische Konzepte hilfreich?, in: Michaela Fink/Reimer Gronemeyer (Hg.), Afrikanische Kindheiten. Soziale Elternschaft und Waisenhilfe in der Subsahara. Bielefeld: transcript Verlag, S. 173–185.

Gürtler, Detlef (2012): Was früher alles besser war, in: der Freitag, 20.12.2012. www.freitag.de/autoren/der-freitag/was-frueher-alles-besser-war.

Henderson, Patricia C. (2012): AIDS, methaphor and ritual: the crafting of care in rural South African childhoods, in: Childhood 20(1), pp. 9–21.

Henderson, Patricia C. (2006): South African AIDS orphans: examining assumptions around vulnerability from the perspective of rural children and youth, in: Childhood 13(3), pp. 303–327.

Hofmann, Eberhard (2016): Namibia: Diskriminierung und Misshandlung von Kindern und Frauen alltäglich, in: Namibiana vom 11.08.2016. https://www.namibiana.de/namibia-information/pressemeldungen/artikel/namibia-diskriminierung-und-misshandlung-von-kindern-und-frauen-alltaeglich.html.

Hornschuh, Jürgen (2019): Mach was!? Los Angeles: creative commons.

Human Development Report (2013): The rise of the south: human progress in a diverse world. NY, USA: United Nations Development Program. http://hdr.undp.org/sites/default/files/reports/14/hdr2013_en_complete.pdf.

Human Rights Watch (1993): Accountabilty in Namibia. Human rights and the transition to democracy. August 1992. An Africa watch report. New York, USA. https://www.hrw.org/sites/default/files/reports/Namibia927.pdf

Illich, Ivan (2003): Entschulung der Gesellschaft. Eine Streitschrift (5. Auflage). München: Beck'sche Reihe.

Illich, Ivan (1992): The message of bapu's hut, in: In the mirror of the past. New York/ London: Marion Boyars, pp. 65–69.

Isiugo-Abanihe, Uche C. (1984): Prevalence and determinants of child fosterage in West Africa: relevance to demography. PSC African Demography Working Paper Series 12.

Keller, Heidi (2009): Die Rolle positiver Emotionen in der frühen Sozialisation. Eine kulturvergleichende Analyse, in: Psychotherapeut 54, S. 101–110.

Klocke-Daffa, Sabine (2001): Wenn du hast, musst du geben: Soziale Sicherung im Ritus und im Alltag bei den Nama von Berseba/Namibia. Münster: Lit Verlag.

Koenen, Eberhard van (2008): Namibias Heilkunde im Wandel. Göttingen/Windhoek: Klaus Hess Verlag.

Kopenawa, Davi/Albert, Bruce (2013): The falling sky: words of a Yanomami shaman. Cambridge: Harvard University Press.

Korczak, Janusz (1967): Wie man ein Kind lieben soll. Göttingen: Vandenhoeck und Ruprecht Verlag.

Kreike, Emmanuel (2004): Re-creating eden. Land use, environment, and society in southern Angola and northern Namibia. Portsmouth: Heinemann Verlag.

Lancy, David (2018): Anthropological perspectives on children as helpers, workers, artisans, and laborers. New York: Palgrave Macmillan Publishers.

Lancy, David (2008): The anthropology of childhood: cherubs, chattel, changelings. Cambridge: Cambridge University Press.

Larsson, Anita (1996): Modernization of traditional Tswana housing: a decade of transformation. Lund: Lund University.

Lee, Franz J. T. (1972): 40.000 Ovambo-Arbeiter streiken gegen Not und Tod, in: Metall 4(11), 15.02.1972. www.franzlee.org.ve/ovambo. html.

Legal Assistance Center (2006): Rape in Namibia – summary report. Gender research and advocacy project. http://www.lac.org.na/ projects/grap/Pdf/rapesum.pdf.

Legal Assistance Centre (2005): Namibian domestic violence and sexual abuse service directory. https://www.lac.org.na/projects/ grap/Pdf/servdir.pdf.

Liebel, Manfred (2020): Decolonizing childhoods. From exclusion to dignity. UK/USA: Policy Press.

Liebel, Manfred (2019): Postkoloniale Dilemmata der Kinderrechte, in: Die Vielfalt der Kindheit(en) und die Rechte der Kinder. Praxisfragen und Forschung im Kontext gesellschaftlicher Herausforderungen. Hg. v. Claudia Maier-Höfer. Wiesbaden: Springer Verlag, S. 21–64.

Manjoo, Rashida/McRaith, Calleigh (2011): Gender-based violence and justice in conflict and post-conflict areas, in: Cornell International Law Journal 44, pp. 11–31. https://www.lawschool.cornell.edu/research/ILJ/upload/Manjoo-McRaith-final.pdf.

McIntosh, Peggy (1988): White privilege unpacking the invisible knapsack. Wellesley College Center for Research on Women (working paper). https://projecthumanities.asu.edu/content/white-privilege-checklist.

Meintjes, Helen/Giese, Sonja (2006): Spinning the epidemic: The making of mythologies of orphanhood in the context of AIDS, in: Childhood 13, pp. 407–430.

Mel, Melisa (2015): Victims and survivors 2. Kaufering: Xlibris.

Melber, Henning (2018): The political economy of Namibia. Rift Valley Institute, UNICEF Esaro Country Paper. https://www.researchgate.net/publication/323639617_The_political_economy_of_Namibia.

Melber, Henning (2016): Revisiting the Windhoek old location (BAB Working Paper 3). https://www.researchgate.net/publication/309415200_Revisiting_the_Windhoek_Old_Location.

Melber, Henning (2015a): Vom sozialen Frieden weit entfernt. Namibia im 24. Jahr seiner Unabhängigkeit, in: Afrikanische Kindheiten. Soziale Elternschaft und Waisenhilfe in der Subsahara. Hg. v. Michaela Fink/Reimer Gronemeyer. Bielefeld: transcript Verlag, S. 99–116.

Melber, Henning (2015b): Gesellschaftspolitische Erkundungen seit der Unabhängigkeit. Frankfurt a.M.: Brandes & Apsel Verlag.

Menke, Chrisoph/Pollmann, Arnd (2007): Philosophie der Menschenrechte zur Einführung. Hamburg: Junius Verlag.

MGECW (2007): National plan of action for orphans and vulnerable
children – Volume 1, 2006–2010. Ministry of Gender Equality and
Child Welfare. Government of the Republik of Namibia, Windhoek, Namibia. https://www.unicef.org/infobycountry/files/NPA-
forOVC-Vol1.pdf.

MGECW (2009a): Minimum standards for residential child care facilities in Namibia. Ministry of Gender Equality and Child Welfare.
Windhoek, Namibia. https://www.pactworld.org/sites/default/
files/RCCF%20Final%20May%2009 %20PDF%20version.pdf.

MGECW (2009b): Draft child care & protection bill – summary. Ministry of Gender Equality and Child Welfare. Government of the
Republic of Namibia. https://www.lac.org.na/projects/grap/Pdf/
ccpa-draft-summary.pdf.

MoHSS (2008): Namibia demographic and health service 2006–07.
Ministry of Health and Social Services. Windhoek. http://dhspro-
gram.com/pubs/pdf/FR204/FR204c.pdf.

Monbiot, George (2008): Small is bountiful (erschienen im »Guardian« am 10.06.2008). https://www.monbiot.com/2008/06/10/
small-is-bountiful.

NAFIN (2019): Malnutrition in Namibia. Namibia Alliance for Improved Nutrition. https://www.unicef.org/namibia/na.Malnutri-
tion_final.pdf.

Namibian Sun (2019): Vulnerable and alone. Child-headed households
are fuelling school dropouts, social experts say, 19.07.2019, von
Jemima Beukes. https://www.namibiansun.com/news/vulnera-
ble-and-alone2019-07-18.

Namibian Sun (2016): Rape, passion killing continue unabated,
28.06.2018, von Gordon Joseph. https://www.namibiansun.com/
news/rape-passion-killing-continue-unabated.

Namibian Sun (2014): Gender-based violence takes centre stage,
28.11.2014, von Gordon Joseph. https://www.namibiansun.com/
news/gender-based-violence-takes-centre-stage.

Namibia Institute for Democracy (2018): Guide to civil society in Namibia. https://www.nid.org.na/images/pdf/ngo_management_training/Guide_to_civil_society_Vol3.pdf.

Namibia Statistics Agency (2017): Namibia inter-censal demographic survey. 2016 report. https://cms.my.na/assets/documents/NIDS_2016.pdf.

New Era (2018): Extreme poverty at 18 % – report, 27.06.2018, von Desie Heita. https://neweralive.na/posts/extreme-poverty-at-18-report.

NPHC (2011): Namibia population and housing census – main report. https://cms.my.na/assets/documents/p19dmn58guram3ottun89rdrp1.pdf.

Odendaal, Willem/Hazam, John (2018): Illegal fencing in communal areas of Namibia. Land governance and tenure security theme. Second national land conference. Legal Assistance Center. http://www.mlr.gov.na/documents/20541/283371/Legal+Assistence+Center+-+Land+Conference+Presentation+by+LAC+v3.pdf/8cbce598-ba16-4e00-b3fa-2b4009fe38e7.

Olsen, Frances (1995): Children's rights: some feminist approaches to the United Nations Convention on the rights of child, in: Childrens Rights and the Law. Ed. by P. Alston et al. Oxford: Oxford University Press.

Oshana Regional Council (2018): Oshana Newsflash. http://www.oshanarc.com/wp-content/uploads/2018/12/ONARC-NEWSLETTER-1.pdf.

Pasolini, Pier Paolo (1989): Freibeuterschriften. Berlin: Verlag Klaus Wagenbach.

Pauli, Julia (2015): Kind unter Kindern. Geschwisterbeziehungen in Fransfontein, Namibia, in: Afrikanische Kindheiten. Soziale Elternschaft und Waisenhilfe in der Subsahara. Hg. v. Michaela Fink/ Reimer Gronemeyer. Bielefeld: transcript Verlag, S. 81–96.

Pendleton, Wade C. (1974): Katutura: a place where we do not want to stay. The social structure and social relationship of people in

an African township in South West Africa. San Diego: San Diego
State University Press.

Penn, Helen (2002): The World Bank's view of early childhood, in:
Childhood (9)1, pp. 118–132.

Pfeifer, Wolfgang (Hg.) (1993): Artikel »Brei« und »Kultur«, in: Etymol-
ogisches Wörterbuch der deutschen Sprache, Bd. 1, 2. Auflage, 2
Bände, Berlin: Adademie Verlag, S. 168 u. 743.

Pletscher, Marianne (2020): 30 Jahre nach der Unabhängigkeit.
https://www.journal21.ch/30-jahre-nach-der-unabhaengigkeit.

Podjavorsek, Peter (2012): Helikopter-Eltern. Werden unsere Kinder
überbehütet? Sendung des Deutschlandradio Kultur, Zeitfragen
vom 03.09.2012. https://www.deutschlandfunkkultur.de/zeit-
fragen-helikopter-eltern-werden-unsere-kinder.media.7f721c-
0675497761960060cd547b539c.pdf (Manuskript der Sendung).

Pupavac, Vanessa (2001): Misanthropy without borders: The international children's rights regime, in: Disasters 25(2), pp. 95–112.

Recknagel, Albert (2010): Die UN-Kinderrechtskonvention zwischen
universellem Anspruch und lokaler Vielfalt, in: Sozialarbeit des
Südens. Band 3: Kindheiten und Kinderrechte. Hg. v. Manfred
Liebel/Ronald Lutz. Oldenburg: Paulo Freire Verlag, S. 67–78.

Schäfer, Rita (2004): Haushaltsdynamiken in Zimbabwe und Namibia,
in: Stichproben. Wiener Zeitschrift für kritische Afrikastudien.
4(7), S. 5–24.

Schooling the World. The White man's last burdon (dokumentary by
Carol Black, 2010). https://schoolingtheworld.org.

Sloterdijk, Peter (2011): Streß und Freiheit. Frankfurt a.M.: Suhrkamp
Verlag.

Spiecker, Johannes (1907): Die Rheinische Mission im Hereroland.
Zugleich Visitationsbericht des Missionsinspektors Pastor Spieker.
Barmen: Missionshaus.

Strauß, Botho (1984): Paare Passanten. Frankfurt a.M.: Suhrkamp
Verlag.

The Economist (2014): The media's focus on violent crimes 2009
– 2013, 2014, 07.03.2020. https://economist.com.na/7507/

community-and-culture/the-media-s-focus-on-violent-crimes-2009-2013-2014.

The Namibian (2019): Severe poverty still haunts Namibians, 02.08.2019, von Charmaine Ngatjiheue. https://www.namibian.com.na/191489/archive-read/Severe-poverty-still-haunts-Namibians.

The Namibian (2018a): Namibian children stunted, wasted, 01.11.2018, von Ndanki Kahiurika. https://www.namibian.com.na/182795/archive-read/Namibian-children-stunted-wasted-%E2%80%93-Mbumba.

The Namibian (2018b): Namibia: Workers struggle with slave wages, 17.08.2018, von Ndapewoshali Shapwanale u. Charmaine Ngatjiheue. https://allafrica.com/stories/201808170384.html.

The Namibian (2015): The exodus of social workers, 20.03.2015, von Theresia Jihenuna. https://www.namibian.com.na/137100/archive-read/The-exodus-of-social-workers.

The Namibian (2014): Close to 90 Erongo school girls pregnant, 22.07.2014, von Paulus Shiku. https://www.namibian.com.na/125896/archive-read/Close-to-90-Erongo-school-girls-pregnant.

The Namibian (2013): Swakop pupil wins essay competition, 24.09.2013, von Rukee Kaakunga. https://www.namibian.com.na/print.php?id=114441&type=2.

The Southern Times (2016): Namibia's NGO's struggeling to survive blames their misfortunes on the upper middle income country status, 08.03.2016, von Timo Shihepo. https://southernafrican.news/2016/03/08/namibias-ngos-struggling-to-survive-blames-their-misfortunes-on-the-upper-middle-income-country-status.

Tönjes, Hermann (1911): Ovamboland. Berlin: Verlag von Martin Warneck.

Tonchi, Victor L./ Lindeke, William A./ Grotpeter, John J. (2012). Historical Dictionary of Namibia. Lanham, MD, USA: Scarecrow press, pp. 330–331.

Trafficking in persons report (2010). Department of State, United States of America. https://2009-2017.state.gov/j/tip/rls/tiprpt/2010//index.htm.

Tutzer, Franz (2019): Hoffnung in Absurdistan. Auf den Spuren von Ivan Illich, in: Was wird aus der Hoffnung? Interdisziplinäre Denkanstöße für neue Formen des Miteinanders. Hg. v. Michaela Fink/Jonas Metzger/Anne Zulauf. Gießen: Psychosozial Verlag, S. 43–58.

Tvedten, Inge (2011): As long as they don't bury me here. Social relations of poverty in a Namibian shantytown. Basel Namibia Studies Series 11. Basel: Basler Afrika Bibliographien.

UNICEF (2011): Children and HIV & AIDS in Namibia. United Nations Children's Fund. https://www.ean.org.na:8080/xmlui/bitstream/handle/123456789/302/UNICEF_Nam_2011_Children_and_AIDS_Namibia.pdf?sequence=1&isAllowed=y.

UNICEF (2010): Children and adolescents in Namibia. United Nations Children's Fund. https://www.unicef.org/sitan/files/SitAn_Namibia_2010.pdf.

UNICEF (2007): Women and children: the double dividend of gender equality. United Nations Children's Fund. https://www.unicef.org/sowc07/docs/sowc07.pdf.

Van Wyk, Anthonie Michael (2019): Investigation the subjective well-being of the informally employed: a case study of day labourers in Windhoek and Pretoria. Dissertation, North-West University Potchefstroom, South-Africa.

Vedder, Heinrich (1934): Das alte Südwestafrika. Südwestafrikas Geschichte bis zum Tode Mahareros 1890. Berlin: Martin Warneck Verlag.

VOA News (2013): Baby dumping reported on rise in Namibia, 04.04.2013, von Kim Lewis. https://www.voanews.com/africa/baby-dumping-reported-rise-namibia.

Wainaina, Binyavanga (2005): How to writhe about Africa, in: Granta Magazine 92. https://granta.com/how-to-write-about-africa.

Wallace, Marion (2011): A history of Namibia: From the beginning to 1990. London: C. Hurst & Co Publishers Ltd. (German edition in 2014).

WFP (2019): Welthungerkarte. World Food Programme. https://docs.wfp.org/api/documents/WFP-0000107776/download/?_ga=2.6240379.97702912.1585149528-687173910.1585149528.

Wiedemann, Charlotte (2019): Der lange Abschied von der weißen Dominanz. München: dtv.

Wiedemann, Charlotte (2020): Vom Weißsein sprechen, in: Le Monde diplomatique, 09.01.2020. https://www.monde-diplomatique.de/!5648371.

Winterfeldt, Volker/Fox, Tom/Mufune, Pempelani (2000): Namibia-Society-Sociology. Windhoek: University of Namibia Press.

Winterhoff, Michael (2008): Warum unsere Kinder Tyrannen werden: Oder: Die Abschaffung der Kindheit (6. Auflage). Gütersloh: Random House/ Gütersloher Verlagshaus.

Yusoff, Kathryn (2018): A billion black anthropocenes or none. Minneapolis: Combined Academic Publishers.

Zimmermann, Martin (2010): The coexistence of traditional and large-scale water supply systems in central northern Namibia, in: Journal of Namibian Studies: History Politics Culture, 7, pp. 55–84. https://namibian-studies.com/index.php/JNS/article/view/73.

(Last access time of all internet sources: 10.02.2021)

Social and Cultural Studies

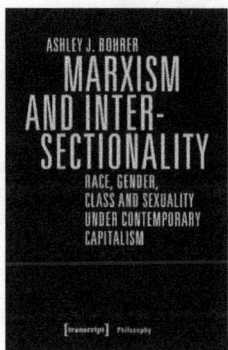

Ashley J. Bohrer
Marxism and Intersectionality
Race, Gender, Class and Sexuality
under Contemporary Capitalism

2019, 280 p., pb.
29,99 € (DE), 978-3-8376-4160-8
E-Book: 26,99 € (DE), ISBN 978-3-8394-4160-2

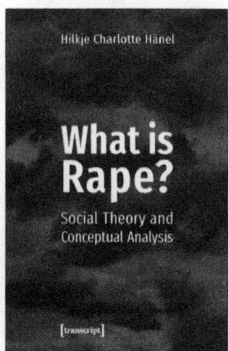

Hilkje Charlotte Hänel
What is Rape?
Social Theory and Conceptual Analysis

2018, 282 p., hardcover
99,99 € (DE), 978-3-8376-4434-0
E-Book: 99,99 € (DE), ISBN 978-3-8394-4434-4

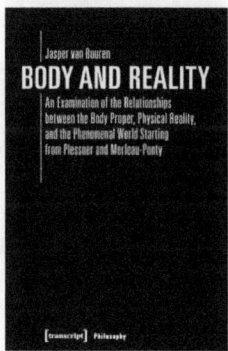

Jasper van Buuren
Body and Reality
An Examination of the Relationships
between the Body Proper, Physical Reality,
and the Phenomenal World Starting from Plessner
and Merleau-Ponty

2018, 312 p., pb., ill.
39,99 € (DE), 978-3-8376-4163-9
E-Book: 39,99 € (DE), ISBN 978-3-8394-4163-3

Social and Cultural Studies

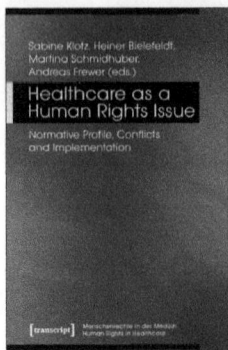

Sabine Klotz, Heiner Bielefeldt,
Martina Schmidhuber, Andreas Frewer (eds.)
Healthcare as a Human Rights Issue
Normative Profile, Conflicts and Implementation

2017, 426 p., pb., ill.
39,99 € (DE), 978-3-8376-4054-0
E-Book: available as free open access publication
E-Book: ISBN 978-3-8394-4054-4

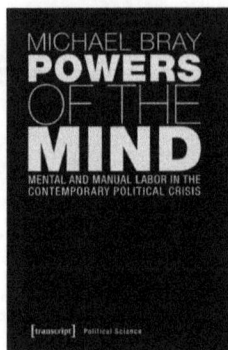

Michael Bray
Powers of the Mind
Mental and Manual Labor
in the Contemporary Political Crisis

2019, 208 p., hardcover
99,99 € (DE), 978-3-8376-4147-9
E-Book: 99,99 € (DE), ISBN 978-3-8394-4147-3

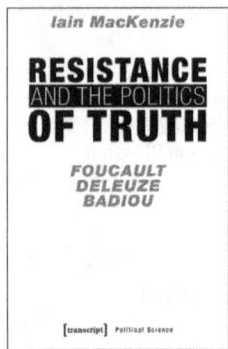

Iain MacKenzie
Resistance and the Politics of Truth
Foucault, Deleuze, Badiou

2018, 148 p., pb.
29,99 € (DE), 978-3-8376-3907-0
E-Book: 26,99 € (DE), ISBN 978-3-8394-3907-4
EPUB: 26,99 € (DE), ISBN 978-3-7328-3907-0

**All print, e-book and open access versions of the titles in our list
are available in our online shop www.transcript-verlag.de/en!**

GPSR Authorized Representative: Easy Access System Europe, Mustamäe tee
50, 10621 Tallinn, Estonia, gpsr.requests@easproject.com

www.ingramcontent.com/pod-product-compliance
Lightning Source LLC
Chambersburg PA
CBHW070110030426
42335CB00016B/2088